G000144558

SHATTERING ILLUSIONS

Shattering
ILLUSIONS

West Indians in British Politics

TREVOR CARTER
with Jean Coussins

Lawrence & Wishart
London

Lawrence and Wishart Limited
39 Museum Street
London WC1A 1LQ

First published 1986

© Trevor Carter, 1986

This book is sold subject to the conditions that
it shall not, by way of trade or otherwise, be lent,
re-sold, hired out or otherwise circulated
without the publisher's prior consent in any
form of binding or cover other than that in
which it is published and without a similar
condition, including this condition, being
imposed on the subsequent purchaser.

Photoset in North Wales by
Derek Doyle & Associates, Mold, Clwyd
Printed in Great Britain by
Camelot Press, Southampton

For my parents, Elene and Clarence Carter.

And in memory of Claudia Jones.

Contents

Acknowledgements

My first thanks are to all those who were kind enough to share their memories, experiences, feelings and thoughts with me about the past, present and future of the black community in Britain. The book could not have been written without the time and support which the following brothers and sisters gave to me: Harold Alleyne, Barbara Beese, Kelvin Caballo, Angela Clement, Jeff Crawford, Frank Crichlow, Gerry Ferdinand, Asquith Gibbes, Bernie Grant, Richard Hart, Lionel Jeffries, Pansy Jeffries, Chris le Maitre, Nat Perez, Cass Philbert, Winston Pinder, Roy Sawh, Billy Strachan, Cleston Taylor, Bobby Thompson and Joan Trotman.

I am also indebted to Kay Beauchamp, Bob Crossman, David Green and Chris Searle for discussions which helped me plan the book; to Burton Louisy, Mark Page, Roy Sanderson and the West Indian Standing Conference for the information they provided; and to Yvonne Collymore for the support she has given me over the years, especially during 1980-1 when I held a fellowship at the Centre for Multi-Cultural Studies at the Institute of Education. Much of the work she collaborated on with me during that year formed the basis for my thoughts in this book on the role of education in the black struggle.

I would also like to thank Buzz Johnson and Billy Strachan for providing me with copies of *Caribbean News* from the 1950s; George Matthews for material from the Communist Party archives; the *Morning Star* library and the Institute of Race Relations, for the use of their facilities and materials.

Bob Marley Music Ltd. B.V., administered in the UK and Eire by Rondor Music (London) Ltd., kindly gave permission to quote the lines from Bob Marley's song, *Buffalo Soldier*, which open the book.

Judith Bennet-Henry, Asquith Gibbes, Lloyd King, Brenda Kirsch and Jeff Rodriguez were all generous enough not only to read the book in draft but to spend a great deal of their already over-committed time and energy discussing it with me and helping to knock it into shape. I am very grateful for their help and advice.

Jean Coussins, my comrade, friend and organiser extraordinaire, was the person who managed to get this book out of my head and onto paper. We worked together on the book for two years; it would have taken several more if I had not had Jean's skill and dedication in organising and recording interviews, editing my notes and drafts and following up research. I, of course, remain responsible for the end result, its political judgements and shortcomings. But I offer my deepest thanks to Jean for her contribution and her understanding.

Finally, I must of course thank my family – Corinne, Dian-Marie, Mick and Lorna – for their support and tolerance at home while I have been writing this book.

1 Introduction

If you know your history
Then you would know where you're coming from,
Then you wouldn't have to ask me,
Who the heck do I think I am?

(Bob Marley, *Buffalo Soldier*)

At the 1984 Notting Hill Carnival, thousands of black people were wearing yellow stickers saying 'Black people support the Miners'. The miners were nearly half way through their year-long strike to save jobs and preserve their communities. The police brutality they encountered on the picket lines shocked them. But it struck a chord with the black community, who had been dealing with police harassment and intimidation every day for decades. A bond of understanding and common purpose between miners and black people was formed.

A month or so later, the TUC's annual conference was held and televised as usual. A single black face was visible. There may have been a handful, but the scores more who should have been there were conspicuous only by their absence.

One place black people have been visible over the past thirty years is at the ballot box, voting Labour. Just before the 1984 Labour Party conference, a document was published which confirmed the loyalty of black people to the Labour Party in elections.[1] In a sample of constituencies held by Labour in the 1979 and 1983 General Elections, over 85 per cent of the black vote went to Labour, compared to only half of the white working-class vote. But black people are now being urged to question this support, ironically by leading black Labour Party activists who are campaigning for black sections within the

Labour Party. Diane Abbott, speaking for the National Black Sections steering committee, warned as the 1984 Labour Party conference began, 'If the Labour Party bungle this issue at Blackpool, they can say goodbye to the black vote.'

Where the black vote is being advised to go instead is not clear. Activists in various fields are, however, beginning to conceive of their voting strength as bargaining power which could be used to advance black rights and equality. The argument has an American flavour to it, and some influence undoubtedly rubbed off from Jesse Jackson's campaign to secure the Democratic Party's nomination for the presidency. A *Caribbean Times* editorial in October 1984 declared: 'The Jesse Jackson factor in the United States has shown what blacks can achieve even in a racist two-party system.' Around the same time, I was surprised to find myself completely isolated in warning of the dangers behind the 'bargaining' strategy, in discussion with other black delegates at a conference organised by the Commission for Racial Equality. The conference itself was relatively insignificant politically, in that it was dealing with internal CRE organisation. But as usual, the real discussion took place in the bar. One brother described how, after twenty years in the Labour Party, he had finally torn up his card in frustration with the racism inside the party. The younger people there shared the same sense of frustration and disgust. They were united in their attraction to the idea of bargaining with any political party who would make a deal.

The warning bells I sounded about the futility of powerless individuals picked off from their community base bargaining with the real power of those who can profit by tokenism seemed to fall on deaf ears. Certain victories have undoubtedly been won in the United States, not least the acceptance by white people of black people as fellow Americans. But the same psychological shift is still a long way from being achieved inside the British and European mentality. The proponents of the bargaining strategy in Britain will comfortably cite Martin Luther King as an example of a black leader who maintained his black consciousness and community base whilst at the same time being in a position to make effective demands on the state. But, from where I stand, quoting a second example always proves difficult. Luther King, admirable though he was, was an historical freak. His successors in the officially acknowledged black leadership have not found it easy to maintain their integrity with their community at the same time as assuming the power of the chosen élite to speak for them.

What all these scenarios add up to is that, after more than thirty years since mass post-war immigration began, black people are still fighting to have their rightful place in' the working class acknowledged. We knew instinctively that we were with the miners, that our struggles were one and the same. We have kept faith, so far, with the Labour Party, despite its responsibility for racist legislation and policies. We have been in the forefront of major industrial disputes such as the NUPE-led health workers' strike in 1982, and of social and political battles around police powers and educational reform. Yet our negotiators and representatives, in the unions and in Parliament, are white. At worst, we are still the 'immigrants', even our British-born children, who some would like to see sent 'home'. At best, we are one of the 'new social forces', together with women, the peace movement and others. We are all meant somehow to help the working class along, as if the working class itself contained no one who was black, female or peace-loving.

The purpose of this book is to argue that the black struggle and the working class struggle overlap and are interdependent. Black people are not merely allies of the working class, they are part of it. A clearer vision of our common goal, which must be socialism, would help to rescue black people from the margins of political activity by redefining the mainstream. This will demand a greater challenge than ever before to the racism harboured within the labour movement and the left generally, where it is all too often ignored or sidestepped, despite the increasing confidence displayed in attacking the racism of other people, whether it be of the government, employers, the police, the judiciary or the media. The task is, of course, two-way: while the white left must become more genuinely anti-racist, black people (as well as white people) must be won for socialism. By writing the struggles of black people into the history of the past thirty years in Britain, this book is intended as a contribution towards the achievement of both these goals.

The chapters which follow trace the relationship between the black community which came to Britain from the Caribbean in the fifties and sixties and the politics of the left. Chapter 2 sets the scene by describing the impact of our arrival in Britain through our eyes. I came in 1954, so the mid-fifties is my starting point, although it was in 1948 that the famous SS *Empire Windrush* brought the first large numbers of West Indian immigrants. The following three chapters pursue the political framework of the West Indian presence in Britain within three distinct phases. The first, from the fifties to 1962, was dominated by the ideology of assimilation or integration. This meant one thing to the establishment and quite another to us. The second, from 1962 to 1976, was characterised by the phrase 'cultural diversity', which represented the state's retreat from a kind of integration that was phoney in the first place, but which it pretended to strengthen by supporting – up to a point – the black community's assertion of its cultural identity in a hostile environment. The third phase, which is still being played out in the eighties, is one where the agenda is finally being acknowledged as having been defined by the black community itself: the fight for equality. The analysis of institutional racism is now inescapable. The challenge, for both black people and white people, is to harness the struggle for race equality with the struggle for sex equality and the working class movement, so that an irreversible shift in society can be won.

By focusing on issues of racism within trade unionism, education and community politics, I want to show that in spite of the history and image of these arenas of struggle having been monopolised by the white left, it is clear when looked at from a black perspective that black peoples' struggles have been instrumental in the development of a strategy to create a new political majority, which can be the only basis for progress towards socialism in Britain. More than that, the battles waged by black people, particularly in the field of education, have opened doors for the whole working class to challenge the values and methods of control which oppress us all. Without either group quite realising it, the black community has been an important catalyst for change.

The left in Britain today is small and fragmented. The Tory government under Margaret Thatcher has put us on the defensive over fundamental issues no one would have dreamed we would be fighting over again in the eighties, such as the right to join a trade union and the existence of the welfare state. It is questionable whether the left is even reproducing itself. The effects of mass youth unemployment means that thousands of young people no longer cross paths with the trade union movement. Socialism in its traditional form can hardly be said to be at the heart of youth culture; feelings of protest and discontent are held by young white people, but then so are the pressures to conform and play it safe in order to increase the chances of getting a slice of the ever-diminishing cake. Most young black people, however, know that because of racism the slice of cake is even more unattainable. They are specialists in protest, yet many are reluctant to identify themselves with the left at all, because of its internal racism and historical neglect of issues of concern to the black community. As the statements from a number of older black activists in this book will show, disillusion with and rejection of the left is not new. The words of the fifties generation of West Indian immigrants are testimony to the tragic waste of talent and commitment of those who could and should have been amongst the highest level of leadership in the labour and trade union movement, were it not for the pressure of racism, both within and outside the movement, which thwarted them and created a cynicism and despair that cannot fail to have been passed on, in some measure, to the next generation.

By producing a glimpse of living history of the fifties immigrants, which is part of what this book sets out to do, their experience and contribution can be made known and validated. This is important not only for that generation itself, but also for the succeeding one. The myth of the generation gap within the black community badly needs to be debunked.

Young black activists and potential activists are obviously susceptible to the belief that our generation let them down by 'selling out', whether to the racist left or the racist establishment, but either way letting the fight for justice and equality for black people fall by the wayside. The combination of personal testimony and political comment I have tried to bring together in this book will, I hope, help to plug the gap of history which a racist society is only too ready to leave open. People are strengthened in struggle if they can feel and know that they are part of an historical process from which they can learn and of which they can be proud. The value of sharing our experience of struggle, and of the younger generation understanding the context of that struggle, is also pragmatic: we have no time to lose. Unity is at a premium. The state has shown how far it can and will go in using race as a tool to divide and rule. Black people's leadership needs to be acknowledged by white people in the interests of unity. This process would be helped by strengthening unity within our own community too. Black people, regardless of their age or sex, are bound together by our culture of resistance, born of slavery, nurtured by colonialism and kept alive and kicking within a democracy that is still racist. This culture of resistance is the thread of continuity which runs through and connects the struggles from generation to generation. Given the goal of socialism, given the channel of organisation, that durable culture of resistance could bind together the kind of alliance with the working class which could bear real fruit.

In *Shattering Illusions* I am drawing on the experiences of only one small section of what we now call 'the black community' in Britain. The experiences and interests of others who came here over the same period, from India, Pakistan and Bangladesh, for example, were not intended to be the subject of this book. There is obviously much which our communities share in common, in terms of prejudice and social and economic discrimination. The Asian communities have also had to struggle over issues such as language and religion, which have not always been seen as so relevant to the West Indian community in personal terms, although they are of course linked politically to our major concerns. In trying to assess the role of the West Indian community over the past thirty years, through the direct experience of myself and fellow activists, I am not putting that above the Asian experience nor ignoring it. But I cannot speak for others. Living history must be written and spoken by the protagonists themselves.

I am also aware that the politics I recount are London-centred and male-dominated. This is a reflection of my own political experience. There are stories and experiences of black women included in this book, but that is not the same as a specifically black women's perspective, which can only come from black women themselves. *The Heart of the Race*, by Beverley Bryan, Stella Dadzie and Suzanne Scafe, published in 1985, is an important history and analysis of black women in Britain.[2]

To complete my excuses and apologies, I must also refer to the term 'West Indian'. As an historical term, it is obviously rooted in slavery and colonialism. A political anachronism. 'Afro-Caribbean' is no more accurate for my purposes and often causes confusion, as it excludes those born in the Caribbean of Indian and Chinese descent. 'Caribbean' on its own is free from the colonialist overtones which beset 'West Indian'. But as this book is about a particular generation of people and relies a great deal on their own words and perceptions, I have used the phrases 'West Indian' and 'West Indies' because those are generally the terms used by the people themselves. When I have used the words 'black' or 'black community', I mean in this context those of us from whatever ethnic or racial background who came to Britain from the West Indies, and our children.

That we define ourselves by the colonialist expression 'West Indian' is ironic, for it belies the extent to which we were aware of colonialism. We arrived in Britain ready-politicised. The level of political consciousness varied, of course, from person to person. But coming from a background where our people had already succeeded in conquering slavery and were currently engaged in fighting colonialism, we had an in-built sense of struggle which gave us a special kind of collective strength. The notion of resistance to white structures is rooted in the West Indian psyche, stemming from the days of slavery. We knew that slavery's abolition had not come about in the way we had been taught at school by colonialist educators, who peddled the line that it was thanks to the hard word of a few liberal, Christian, good-natured white people. It was the result of our own peoples' continuous resistance and struggle. Books such as *Capitalism and Slavery* by Eric Williams and *Black Jacobins* by C.L.R. James have documented this analysis.[3]

Those of us who came to Britain in the fifties had grown up in a period of sustained political activity at home. During the twenties and thirties the economic recession which hit Europe and metropolitan countries also swept the colonies. The English-speaking Caribbean moved into a period of anti-colonial unrest. The foundations of the modern trade union movement and political parties were laid. The focus of activity was initially on general bread-and-butter issues, but the struggle moved on quickly towards the goals of adult suffrage and political independence. This movement touched everyone's lives and a strong sense of solidarity bound us together in the face of an easily identifiable enemy, British imperialism. Leaders like Bustamante and Norman W. Manley in Jamaica, Tubal Uriah Buzz Butler in Trinidad, Eric Gairey in Grenada and Cheddi and Janet Jagan in British Guyana were all household names in the West Indies.

It was not only in the field of political agitation that the might of colonial oppression was felt. Christian religious organisations and churches with strong African traditional elements were also banned. In many cases, it was only after independence that people were allowed legally to practice their religion in comparative freedom.

It is not surprising, then, that when we came to Britain, we considered the left and the labour movement to be our natural allies. As one brother put it to me, 'We came looking for politics.'

It would, however, be naïve to give the impression that because we had an understanding of colonialism and some of us felt we were in the thick of politics, we had not also been trapped by colonialist ideology and that our heads were not as confused as hell in regarding white people with both reverence and contempt at the same time. We were taught to know our place at home and to regard England as the 'mother country', the pinnacle of civilization. The desire to come here was above all in search of more and better education. Very few of us came with the intention of staying for good. Most – men and women – intended to study, or work and study, then to go home after three to five years.

I came in 1956. I saw education as a means to move out of poverty. So I came to work and study. We had seen plenty of rags-to-riches films at home and I thought England would give me that opportunity to work my way through college. My father told me England was the seat of learning. We sang 'Land of Hope and Glory' and 'Rule Britannia' at school. I had a British passport and felt I belonged. I respected white people ... if I was arguing with a friend, we would go to a white man to decide who was right. We would both immediately accept his point of view. I knew white people were the bosses and so to better myself I had to emulate the white man. At school we read Trollope, Shakespeare and Dickens. We looked at Europe as the epitome of knowledge – and power. At the same time, I had a sixth sense that something was wrong, but I accepted it. Our parents could not foresee the day when we would stand up and say we were equal. So they taught us how to cope with our situation, but not how to combat it. As I got older, I accepted there were certain occupations I could not enter, so I set my sights low. Every step of the way I needed the approval of the white man. On reflection I realize I grew up in a state of confusion. We didn't get education, we only got schooling. I decided to get out of the ghetto by coming to England. I planned to stay here three to five years.

I was sent by my parents to do nursing. I intended to stay four years. I was starry-eyed. I had always looked at England as where you got your directions from. Most of our teachers were from England or Canada. The church people were from Scotland. They all seemed to have knowledge and be sophisticated. At the same time, I thought of white people as difficult and inclined to be snobbish, but I looked to England for leadership. We had felt

sympathy for them during the war. I felt I wanted some
excitement. The Caribbean was dead and I wanted out.

Education was my reason for coming. I thought of Britain as a
place of intellectual development, a place where people wrote
books and did things at a level we couldn't. It was a nice feeling to
know I was coming to England. I felt I was programmed to go,
and then return home afterwards. I intended to stay for four years.
To me it was going to be a higher form of life. I was conscious that
my colour had put me in a certain position in society. I knew I
couldn't get a job in a bank after school and only in certain
departments of the civil service. I was aware of my mother's strong
sense of grievance that her children would not be able to achieve
certain things.

I arrived at Plymouth on Sunday 16 April 1954 on the SS
Columbie, after sailing for sixteen days with several hundred
immigrants, mainly from Trinidad and Guyana. Like many
others, I had always had the idea of coming to England to
study, but my mind had been firmly made up after spending
several weeks in New Orleans and witnessing the degree of
state-organised and legally sanctioned racism in the United
States.

The most memorable aspect of the journey itself was the
sharing of dreams of the future in the 'mother country'. Very
few talked of making money. Those who did talked about
making just enough to return home and set up a small
business.

What we didn't know until opening the newspapers on 2
January 1985, when government papers were released to the
public under the 30-year rule, was that even as we were
arriving full of hope in 1954, the Conservative government was
already trying to devise a means of passing discriminatory
immigration laws to cope with 'the problem of coloured
immigrants'. The first post-war arrivals on the *Empire
Windrush*, 492 Jamaicans, who were nearly all ex-servicemen,
had already experienced a 'welcome' that was somewhat
different from the warmth with which they had been received a
few years earlier when they had enlisted in the fight against
fascism. The debate on immigration began. By 1954, we now

know, when 10,000 of us arrived in one year, certain members of the Cabinet were approaching a state of panic. One said there was now 'no limit to the numbers likely to come here'. Another spoke of complaints being made to MPs by their constituents of 'large numbers of coloured people ... living on National Assistance or the immoral earnings of white women'. These discussions led eventually to the Commonwealth Immigration Act in 1962 ... by which time many illusions had indeed been shattered.

Notes

1. Labour Party, *Black People and the Labour Party*, 1984.
2. B. Bryan, S. Dadzie and S. Scafe, *The Heart of the Race*, Virago, 1985.
3. E. Williams, *Capitalism and Slavery*, University of North Carolina Press, 1942; C.L.R. James, *Black Jacobins*, Vintage Books, New York, 1963.

2 Mixed Feelings

> We saw all these English people pushing trolleys. I said to the guy next to me, 'Who are these people?' He said they were porters. I said, 'White people, doing this sort of job?' He said, 'Yes, it's their country, they've got to work.' It suddenly clicked. To be quite honest, I was surprised and flabbergasted. Genuinely surpised and taken aback. Porters ... and calling me 'sir' and being nice and helpful. I couldn't believe it. I thought, is this England, with them doing this job – and they're supposed to be so clever and they're ruling *us*?

The vast majority of white people with whom we had contact in the West Indies were part of the ruling class. Our teachers, our employers, our political and economic controllers, all represented Britain and had given us virtually the only picture of Britain and the British we had.

The first shock when we arrived was to see white men working as dockers and porters. We didn't expect white people to be doing those kinds of jobs or providing a service for black people. Yet there they were, not only willing to carry our suitcases, but also waiting for a tip.

A friend who landed in Liverpool remembers the first shock of seeing white people scrubbing floors: 'I had never seen them work before.' One of the first images which jolted me soon after arriving was the sight of the red, raw and swollen hands of charladies: I had been so strongly conditioned to equate white skin with beauty that I was shocked. Not only were we surprised to find a white working class, but astonished to see anything which did not conform to the picture of well-being and advanced civilisation with which we had grown up.

I wasn't prepared for a white working class. But more than that – I wasn't prepared for the baseness I saw, for the sight of prostitution in Piccadilly, or for the old, cold houses.

My first thought was that England looked like one big funeral. Everyone in grey and black. Factory chimneys and grim houses.

Britain in the Fifties

What was everyday life like for these ordinary working people we were so surprised to find? West Indian immigrants had to survive in appalling conditions, but we did not have a monopoly on hardship. The Britain we had come to, sure of opportunities and eventual prosperity, was of course a deeply divided society, with its extremes of rich and poor, the rulers and the oppressed. The mid-fifties was the time when the people were told they had 'never had it so good'. The post-war period had brought the welfare state based on the Beveridge Plan of 1942, which was meant to provide 'security without want' – an unachieved goal, but nevertheless representing then an extent of social security which did not exist in the West Indies. The level of child support through the tax-benefit system was at its peak, relative to pensions and earnings. Food rationing ended and the 1954 Budget held the rate of income tax steady for the second year running. The General Election in May 1954 returned the Conservatives to power with an increased majority.

But this apparent stability concealed an acute poverty which was still widespread. The trend towards equality in economic terms was superficial and short-lived. There were already nearly half a million people dependent on supplementary benefit by 1948 and the numbers have risen steeply ever since. In 1954, the top 1 per cent of wealth-holders owned 80 per cent of all personally held company shares and the top 5 per cent owned 96 per cent. By the end of the fifties the distribution of income and wealth was again as unequal as it had been in 1937.

Thousands of families in the inner city lived in crisis conditions. A front page story in the *Daily Worker* a couple of months after I arrived in 1954 told of a London bus driver, his wife and five children, who were living in one room. They had been on the housing list since 1943. Another story reported ten adults and three babies sharing a single tap and an old stone sink. These were typical conditions in East London. During that period, the organised working class, through tenants' groups and trade unions, together with the Communist Party, were embattled in a fight against the government's Housing Repairs and Rents Bill. This law was to give a licence to private landlords to impose rent increases and to allow property-owning companies to make a financial killing.

The post-war period saw the return of inequalities which had been temporarily and artificially suspended during the war. When meat rationing was abolished in July 1954, for example, the government hailed it as 'freedom day'. The effect in practice, however, was the rapid establishment of one diet for the rich and another for the poor. Prices rocketed. The cost of steak doubled within one week. There was a housewives' 'meat strike' in protest, but with very limited success. The fifties also put women back in the home, when their jobs were handed back to men and their role in the labour market summarily declared superfluous. 'Full employment' meant full male employment. Nurseries which had opened during the war were closed down and women were pressurised into thinking their fulfilment lay once again exclusively in home-making. Theories of 'maternal deprivation' made those who where still forced to work to make ends meet feel guilty about doing so. Professional women, mainly single, in the civil service and teaching, were stepping up their campaign for equal pay during the fifties. But the lot of most working-class women with no trade union protection to support them consisted of cleaning, sewing and washing jobs and, like many men, the dreadful exploitation of piece work in factories.

Trade union membership had been rising fast ever since the end of the war. Nationally, the energies of the trade union movement were being directed into several major campaigns, including opposition to German re-armament and support for national military service to be reduced from two years to one.

Another campaign, interesting to look back on in the light of today's major national issues, was against the 'sham of civil defence'. Centred in Coventry, this campaign sought to expose the hypocrisy and waste of resources involved in taking preventive measures to resist the outcome of an atom or hydrogen bomb attack.

How was this section of British society – the labour movement – likely to respond to the new wave of West Indian immigrants? Many of us soon discovered that we could not always count on support or solidarity from our natural allies. Peter Fryer in his book *Staying Power* has documented the resistance of trade unions to the employment of black workers in the post-war period.[1] In Liverpool in 1948 the anti-black policies of the National Union of Seamen led to racist riots. In Bristol only a boycott of buses by black people forced the bus company to change its policy of not employing black bus crews. Several unions adopted a quota system, restricting black workers to 5 per cent of the workforce. There were many one-day strikes by Transport and General Workers' Union members against the employment of black transport workers. Even the respected union principle of 'last in, first out' for redundancies was subverted where there were black workers, whose place in the pecking order was naturally deemed to be below that of 'last in'. The ease with which this particular trade union tradition was varied when qualified by racism was later to be seen mobilised at the expense of women also.

Thanks to the leadership of some white trade union activists, together with their commitment to anti-racism gained through struggle, there are also some victories to record alongside the catalogue of discriminatory practices. A white Communist shop steward in London during the fifties remembers with delight how the railwaymen organised to fight racism, in and out of work, often after a painful process of confronting their own personal racist feelings. His recollections provide good examples of how the presence and pressure of black workers could stimulate greater workplace solidarity than had been known before, and raise political consciousness across the board.[2]

When the first black porter was recruited at Kings Cross goods yard, the goods workers downed tools. When seventeen black trainee shunters were employed at Camden goods yard there too was an immediate stoppage and threats of a strike. The same thing happened when black workers were to be trained as guards. The white workers often found an alternative to overt racism as their justification for such action: 'lack of industrial knowledge which endangered the safety of indigenous workers' was a frequent excuse. Another, previously well rehearsed within the trade union movement when women were trying to break into sectors of skilled and craft work, was that an influx of workers to meet a labour shortage put the strength of the union's bargaining power at risk. (The hypocrisy of this excuse was exposed by the fact that despite the presence of many non-trade unionists in the fifties amongst the railwaymen, *every* black worker joined the union.)

Management too, despite the urgent need for labour, could not resist drawing the racist line somewhere. Tony Gilbert remembers a confrontation between management and progressive shop stewards over the duties assigned to black guards. Guards' jobs needed to be filled, but the stewards insisted that if they supplied the labour then the black guards would participate in all duties – including operating the royal trains, which left from Euston. Management instantly dropped their demands, preferring to be under-staffed than allow black workers on the royal trains.

Another memory illustrates the feelings of solidarity and unity amongst the workers, inspired by a commitment to anti-racism:

> Shunting is a dangerous job and it is impossible to work in fog. One such foggy night we were in our guards and shunters cabin, waiting for a heavy mist to lift, when in burst a man we didn't know. He ignored the white shunters and railed at the black ones. 'Where do you think you are, in the jungle? Get out there and do your job.' I represented guards and shunters and asked, 'Who are you?' 'An outside inspector,' he replied, 'to report on some of the nonsense that goes on here.' 'Is that so?' he was told. 'In that case, you can report that there will be no more work done here tonight,

tomorow and perhaps for quite a while, unless there is an apology for your behaviour which is acceptable to us all.' He stormed out. There was a great cheer from all of us and we prepared to brew a jug a tea for what might be a long stay. It wasn't too long. Euston [headquarters of British Rail] called me to the telephone for our version. In a short while, back crawled the 'outside inspector' with an abject apology. We worked joyfully for the rest of the night shift. It is a great feeling when workers together declare 'no racism here'.

The Camden railwaymen took their struggle outside the workplace too. The 'colour bar' in the pubs in the surrounding area was their target. They organised protests, challenged breweries and took on the licensing authorities. It was slow, hard work, but they drew on their strength as organised workers as well as individuals:

Camden Railwaymen's Social Club cancelled orders for all the brewery's stocks and told them officially, through the National Union of Railwaymen, that we would call on all railwaymen's clubs in London to do likewise. Webster (who, with his brothers, ran the pubs in question) was removed and the next we knew he was vending gaming machines. His brothers caved in and the message was received by other public houses and they were forced to find other ways to make black customers unwelcome.

By the mid-fifties, some unions were beginning to produce general statements against racial discrimination. The 1955 Trades Union Congress passed unanimously the following resolution proposed by the Civil Service Clerical Association:

This Congress condemns all manifestations of racial discrimination or colour prejudice, whether by governments, employers or workers. It urges the General Council to lose no opportunity to make the trade union attitude on this issue perfectly clear and to give special attention to the problems emerging in this country from the influx of fellow workers of other races with a view to removing causes of friction and preventing exploitation.

Apparently well intentioned policies like this, however, were just so many fine words to the majority of black workers. National policies are sometimes difficult to translate into practice at the grass-roots level and the daily experience of black people reflected more the real antagonism of trade unionists than the sympathy of official policy.

The education system in Britain, one of the biggest magnets which had drawn us here, also turned out to be something of a shock in reality. In 1954 there was still some discontent amongst Tories about the raised school-leaving age, which had gone up from fourteen to fifteen after the war. One Tory MP attacked the measure saying that it produced 'hundreds of bored and bolshie children'. It was a few more years yet before children from West Indian families entered the education system in substantial numbers. Their parents had come to Britain in the belief that education was the key to upward mobility. 'I came believing one hundred per cent in the English education system,' said one Trinidadian. But the educational process which was already failing to help white working class children break barriers was hardly likely to be able to reflect or respond to the interests of West Indian families. During the mid-fifties, studies culminating in the Crowther Report of 1959 demonstrated the extent to which working class children, even if they made it to grammar school, left by the age of sixteen.[3] Brian Jackson and Dennis Marsden in their 1962 book *Education and the Working Class* described it plainly as a 'class wastage'.[4] They concluded:

> Middle-class families are in so many ways insured against failure by virtue of their class position; and any form of *nominally academic* selection will, in effect, be a form of *social* selection ... [Selection] is not an event that happens and ends suddenly at 11 plus or 18 plus. It is a process that is at work all the time from the moment the child enters school to his final leaving: a gentle shaking of the sieve, with now and again one or two big jerks ... No overhaul of the present system (though not to be scorned) will go far enough to meet what we take to be the major problem facing state education. That problem, quite bluntly, is how can we open education to the working class?

By the mid-sixties, it was to become clear that the philosophy and practice of British education also meant built-in failure for black children too.

First Impressions in the Inner City

The train journey from Plymouth to Paddington was remarkable for the sight of the English countryside with its well ordered and laid out farms. The vast majority of us never saw the countryside again for years, as our lives were to be trapped in the inner-city areas. At Paddington Station hundreds of our own people would be waiting to meet friends and relatives. Nevertheless, many were disappointed at finding no one to greet them and had to make their own way to the only address they had. Innocent of the size of the country and the distances between the main towns and cities, some showed taxi drivers addresses in Birmingham and Manchester and spent their last pound on the fare there from London. Others, without an address or a contact, ended up being charged an exhorbitant sum for one night's stay in a dingy basement room with ten to fifteen others. Some women arrived only to find that the partner with whom they had come to settle had either moved house or was living with someone else.

Despite dreams of achievement in 'the motherland', we did not come with the illusion that life would be easy at first. Many of us had relatives who had gone to the United States and knew that they had had to face hard work and underemployment, particularly if they were unskilled. What we were unprepared for in Britain was racism. We knew that it operated – and was even legalised – in the States; indeed, some of us had chosen to come to Britain precisely because we believed racism did not exist here.

I had no notion of racism before I came to England. I didn't know the word.

I thought there would be racism because Britain was an old imperial country. But I didn't feel racism represented the majority of the people.

I was surprised at first – deflated, shocked and humiliated. I couldn't believe that a charlady could think herself better than me.

We didn't speak about racism to each other. Your feelings when confronted by racism were modified by the perspective of planning to stay only three to five years. We couldn't cope with it, but we learned how to deal with it.

The black religious community received a particularly harsh jolt from the racism they found in the church, the one place where, above all, they expected to be welcomed and treated equally.

All the believers, from whatever denomination, came here thinking that England was actually an extension of what they believed. But as our numbers increased within different church congregations, it seemed that we had become an embarrassment to the white believers. We didn't really know how to deal with this, as we had no experience of fellowship with white believers, coming from mainly black congregations in the Caribbean. Some of us set up an organisation called *Buffer*. It was decided that we should present ourselves at the nearest church and encourage our members to go there. We felt that would be a nice gesture and that the church would welcome us. But the first Sunday we went, the vicar told us that our lusty singing, although commended, was perhaps a little too strong for their approach to worship. It was less than subtly hinted that if we wanted to return, we should not come back in such large numbers. This was a real shock.

It was traumatic. We couldn't understand why we were received so coldly. We thought we were coming to brethren who cared. After a time, we withdrew and started to meet in our homes instead. Most of the Pentecostal churches have grown out of the network of house meetings.

Finding Somewhere to Live

Imagine our shock, the day after arriving at Paddington Station, when we began searching for somewhere to live, to see the signs saying 'No blacks, no dogs' on almost every shop window or front door advertising rooms to let. Sometimes the sign wasn't there, but we got the message anyhow: a friend of mine rang the doorbell of a house which advertised rooms to let, only to get a bucket of cold water poured over him from an upstairs window.

In the inner-city areas to which we were drawn by the light manufacturing industries, we competed with the Irish and others for bedsit accommodation. Council housing was not an option for us: most were single and in our twenties. But even the families with children could not get council housing because of the residence qualification.

Most private landlords did not want black tenants any more than the local authority. Often their insulting signs in the window included 'No Irish' and 'No children' along with the proscribed blacks and dogs. The rents for the flats and rooms we did get were grossly inflated, sometimes four times the amount charged to white tenants. 'Black tax' it was called. One Guyanese man remembers the insult and humiliation:

> I paid the equivalent of £2.70 a week to rent a room, when the average wage was around £5. But the worst thing was the feeling of sheer panic as Friday loomed and you had been told to be out by the end of the week. Trekking round notice boards, wasting money on phone calls, hearing the same old story time after time: 'The room has just gone.' I realised racism was getting to me as a person and undermining my confidence when I went for a room once and turned back when I saw the house – it looked too good. I thought, that's not for black people, they won't have me, and didn't even bother knocking on the door.

The combination of financial and racist exploitation by private landlords led many immigrant families to try to buy their own homes, with all the sacrifice that entailed. This was no easy task either. To get a mortgage, earnings had to be over a certain amount. Since most black people were in low-paid jobs, they were automatically disqualified by the reputable mortgage companies. The few who earned enough to qualify found themselves discriminated against in the type of property offered, if they were offered any at all. The difficulty of getting a mortgage through normal channels forced many black people into the jaws of loan sharks, who charged incredibly high interest rates and stipulated a shorter than usual repayment period. Often the only way they could make their exhorbitant repayments was by becoming landlords themselves and letting out some of their rooms, in many cases to other black people. It was, therefore, sometimes necessary to charge fairly high rents to recoup enough for the mortgage. This provided an easy diversion for 'public opinion' and the press, who would point to black landlords 'exploiting' their own people, as if that nullified the more widespread racism of the housing market. An alternative to the loan shark was a request to your employer to provide false documentary evidence showing that your wages were higher than they actually were, in order to qualify for a regular mortgage. We did it through lack of choice. The employers did it because it kept us working for them.

Finding Work

Compared to accommodation, finding a job was easy. By 1954, post-war West Indian immigration had been going on for six years. By 1958, 125,000 of us had arrived since the end of the war. Special recruitment campaigns by employers were targeted on particular West Indian communities. London Transport began recruiting labour from Barbados in 1956 and by 1966 the demand was such that the exercise was extended to Trinidad and Jamaica. Hotel and restaurant workers and nurses were also expressly sought from the West Indies. The problem facing skilled workers (which nearly half the men and over a quarter of the women were) was that only unskilled manual work was made available to us.

> I arrived on a Sunday night. On the Monday morning I was taken to the Labour Exchange to go through all the formalities. I remember very clearly the cold stare given to me by the man behind the counter when I told him that I was interested in a job as a tracer in a drawing office. The reason I chose that job was because I had done about three years of evening classes doing a City and Guilds course in architectural draughtsmanship and although I had no formal drawing office practice, I was confident that I could at least pull lines because of the experience I had in

drawing basic plans for my father, who had been a building contractor. The job vacancy pages of the daily and evening papers were full of thousands of vacancies for this kind of job. But the Labour exchange clerk paid no attention to my request and went straight to a filing cabinet labelled either manual workers or labourers.

Often you didn't have to wait until you got inside the Labour Exchange to discover you were labelled as unskilled, regardless of your qualifications or experience. The man on the gate would direct you automatically to the entrance for unskilled labour. A second door for would-be clerical workers – male ones anyway – was closed to us on sight. The women fared slightly better in getting office work. The following account from a Guyanese friend illustrates the lengths to which employers and their personnel staff would go to prevent black recruitment to 'white collar' jobs. He remembers:

I tried to get a job as a counter clerk with the Post Office. There was a written test, arithmetic and so on. I finished it quickly, in about ten minutes. I got it all right and the guy seemed really angry. Then there was an oral test. He tried to trick me but again I got everything right. Desperate to catch me out somehow, he then asked me what a 'tanner' was. I guessed and said it was a ten pound note. I could see the joy on his face – he'd got me at last and said I couldn't have the job. I felt really smashed and shattered.

For those who had friends or family here already and were therefore spared the frustration and humiliation of flat or room hunting, finding a job was often the setting for the first confrontation with racism. One such Trinidadian recalls:

The first time I felt there was something wrong with this country was when I went to the Colonial Office about a job. They knew about my qualifications but could only offer me a packing job in a factory for £7 a week. I took it, thinking it would do for the time being. Then the man interviewing me said something about us all coming here behaving badly and he hoped I wouldn't be walking out on the job. My temper was never raised in years like it rose there. I felt like giving the man my right hand. He had been talking down to me in a way I could never have imagined. I just couldn't understand being spoken to in that way – as if I had come here to beg.

The unskilled jobs many of us found were with small manufacturing firms, often Jewish-owned. The Jewish community had a much more sympathetic attitude towards West Indians than we found in general. They understood from their own experience the racism we had to face. London was littered with small workshop industries, which were desperate for unskilled and semi-skilled labour at a time when skilled white workers could take advantage of post-war full (male) employment and go for jobs with better pay and working conditions.

My first job was with a small manufacturer of optical lenses. I was relegated to one of the less skilled jobs, but was glad to be working. The conditions were terrible. There were no canteen facilities – just a woman who made tea and provided buttered rolls and jam. There were no more than a hundred workers, the majority of whom were Turkish or Maltese. There were also some very bitter Polish people. My mate and I were the only two West Indians. There was a kind of affinity between us and some of the other immigrant workers, because we were in the same position. There were very few white English workers. They were either young people doing their first job, or older men and women with a few years to go before retirement. The movements of the older men's bodies were synchronised with their machines. They were humourless, gaunt and often seemed shell-shocked. They never spoke about their wartime experiences, they just looked unhappy and defeated. I couldn't detect any social contact between them. The place was a three-storey building with a dingy basement. My job was in the basement, needless to say. It was only after I left that job, six months later, that I realised the firm did not observe the basic health and safety regulations. Part of the process in grinding the rough glass into the polished finish was to put it into a mould and pour over hot pitch. The pitch was kept in a container on the workbench on a constantly burning gas ring. We stood to earn a bonus if we exceeded a certain number of lenses produced each day. As the basic wage was so low, there was always an incentive to work fast despite the hazards. Once I became less than careful in pursuit of my few extra shillings and burned both hands in the hot pitch. I was given a couple of days off and then given another job to do until my hands were well enough to return to my original job.

On another occasion, my palm was swollen and painful. I went to the nearest hospital and had to have a minor operation to remove a piece of glass. There was no real sympathy from the management, or anyone else for that matter.

I was seen as a very odd person by most of the people at work, especially the English. I was probably the first West Indian they had met. My attitudes must have jarred against their stereotyped views of black people. For a start, I read the *Daily Worker* and *The Times*, while they mainly read the two popular tabloids, the *Daily Mirror* and the *Daily Sketch*, with a few reading the *Daily Express*. Their chief interest in the papers was the sports section. They spent most of the time picking winners from the horse racing pages and doing their pools coupons. Inevitably, I had a much better grasp of national and international events than they had. My experience was different and I saw the world from a completely different point of view. There was a paradox here: the explanation they gave for reading the tabloids was that they reflected the working class, whereas *The Times* reflected the views of the ruling class. On the surface that was partly true, but the fact remained that *The Times* had a much more detailed coverage of the real social and political issues. No amount of persuasion could make my fellow workers change their minds.

Although our views differed, I found there was a natural, if superficial, sympathy towards the black people in South Africa and to elements of the national liberation struggles that were taking place all over the world. Nevertheless, their views were informed largely by the way the popular media presented the facts. The national liberation movement in Kenya, for example, was depicted by the description of the Mau Mau as a band of ruthless, uncivilised, barbarous savages led by Jomo Kenyatta who was labelled by the then Governor General as the 'leader of darkness and death'. On one hand, therefore, I found in my workmates a pride in their working class origins and a healthy dislike for anything that appeared to be middle class, yet by and large they accepted the ruling class views presented to them through the popular media.

Although we may have established reasonably friendly relationships with our early workmates, many an incident occurred which brought home to us the unexpected depth of racism in the consciousness and attitudes of the English people with whom we thought we had a degree of friendship.

In my firm the cleaner would ask different people to help lift out the heavy dustbins into the streets every evening. When my turn came I did it without any question. I accepted that this was how things were organised and that there was an element of equality. I also accepted that I had to undertake work that I considered beneath my dignity for the time being. I noticed, however, that my turn was becoming much more frequent. One evening, I refused. The cleaner got very angry and complained to the foreman who upbraided me. In the argument that ensued, I very quickly realised that both the cleaner and the foreman automatically assumed that not only would I accept the task of taking out the dustbins but also believed that I was the person to do it. This was my first lesson in racism and how it affects the mind of every white person, no matter what their social position.

My first job was with British Rail at King's Cross Station. I was the only black. I played cricket in the club for the works team. They made me feel like a little mascot. One weekend, we went to play against the Loughton team and they invited me back. Two weeks later, on my own, I thought I'd follow up the invitation and went to visit their social club again. The place fell silent the second I walked in. They were obviously shocked to see me and I felt rotten. So I stayed half an hour, then made an excuse to leave, saying I had just been passing.

I had got friendly with this white guy at work. We often had a drink together, he seemed really sympathetic and we talked about all sorts of things. Then one day he told me he was getting married. I said he'd have to tell me the date so I could get a new suit. He shifted about and seemed really uncomfortable. I couldn't work out what the matter was at all, but finally he managed to tell me I wouldn't be welcome at the wedding. I couldn't believe it, we were such good friends. He said it wasn't to do with him, but his girlfriend's mother wouldn't like a black man there. I could tell that was an excuse and couldn't bring myself to be friendly with him again. That was the end of it for me, I felt hurt.

Although jobs were easy to come by, even if they weren't of the calibre we expected, there were two features of West Indian employment which made us vulnerable and added to the general racial prejudice we had to live with. The first was the overwhelming pressure of working and studying at the same time. Those of us who had the anchor of political and trade union involvement at least found a personal network of solidarity which kept us sane, even though being an activist as well as a worker and student meant even more demands on our time. But there were many immigrants whose personal isolation was acute. This plus physical exhaustion through lack of sleep due to working all day and studying all night (or the other way round) pushed some to their limits. To white society, the symptoms of this pressure must have fuelled the stereotype of the crazy black man. For those of us who understood, it was still often no easier to get close to the ones who suffered.

During my stay at my first workplace, another West Indian – a Jamaican – joined the firm. For some reason, which I was later to understand, he kept himself to himself. Like so many of us, he was doing a job way below his capabilities and was attending evening classes to prepare himself to do law. His work and his studies obviously took up all his time and this had its effects on him. I noticed that he talked to himself incessantly and appeared to be unhappy and lonely. Not being able to take it any longer, I approached the brother and extended a hand of friendship. He looked at me and without uttering a word he raised his arm and attempted to stab me with a piece of metal he was using. I was surprised by the force and power he used. I reacted swiftly and escaped with only a blow to my shoulder. When I looked at him again he was muttering that I should leave him alone. I was struck by the agony and anger on his face. I realised he was ill and spoke to the manager, who could not have cared less. The brother was performing his mindless task and that was all that mattered to the firm. A few weeks later the firm was forced to sack him – he had seriously injured a cleaner. This whole episode taught me three lessons. First, the the firm was fundamentally exploitative and had no concern for its employees' health. Second, that no attention was paid to my observations as another black person who was trying, in everybody's interest, to explain something I intuitively understood. Third, I saw the effect of the pressures on the mental well-being of the black immigrant trying to make a superhuman effort in a hostile environment, without the natural community support that we all depend on to survive.

The second, though related, feature of our employment conditions, was the problem of being underemployed, relative to our skills. This could often lead to trouble in factories where we were unaware of the conventions which unorganised workers adopted to protest collectively against their bosses and working conditions. One of these conventions was to spin out your tasks for as long as possible. One Trinidadian who worked in a small firm ruled by its owner in a benign dictatorial way did not understand this and ended up being sacked literally for doing his job properly. He was a very efficient worker and never learned that the one thing you never did was to complete your work. He would get through his tasks, then stand around doing nothing. The other workers tried to convince him that this was not in anyone's interest, because it showed them up and undermined the only form of action they had to take a stand against the boss. The brother didn't understand and became very unpopular. The foreman must have realised what was happening but gave no advice. Instead he picked on the man and generally harassed him. This eventually led to violent arguments – and the sack.

Social Life

To begin with, just finding our way round in London could be a problem. We were shocked by the hostility of people who wouldn't give a straight answer to a straight question. Small, everyday incidents made such an alarming impression that today, thirty years later, every word and detail of a brief exchange can be recalled. On my second day here, I was looking for the underground station near to where I lived. I approached a policeman and began to ask in a way that seemed natural to me, 'Pardner, can you tell me where ...' That's as far as I got. He looked at me coldly in the eyes, very unfriendly, and said, 'Listen here, I am no partner of yours and in future when you see a policeman in uniform you address him as officer – none of this partner business.' Around the same time, I was on a bus and when I thought I was nearly at my destination I came downstairs and said to the bus conductor, 'Pal, could you tell me if I am near ...' I can't remember finishing the sentence. He said, 'Look, I'm no fucking pal of yours,' and disappeared down the bus.

A common incident in the streets which underlined the way we were seen as oddities, if not savages, was children constantly stopping to ask the time. If you told them in the ordinary way, they would show real disappointment: they wanted us to look up into the sky and tell them the time by the sun. A friend of mine tried doing this once and the children leaped up and down with delight, thinking they had spoken to their idea of a witchdoctor from the jungle.

Social life outside the home was non-existent for many West Indians in London. It was slightly better in Brixton, where large groups of Jamaicans settled and formed a fairly close knit community. On the whole, however, we were forced to develop the habit of holding parties at home, since so many pubs (where most white working class social life took place) were effectively barred to us because of the publicans' racist attitudes or rules. (One friend of mine found a pub where they agreed to serve him, but only if he brought his own glass.) It was not long before the pattern of entertaining ourselves at home, although imposed on us by a racist society, was twisted round and seen by white people as a stereotyped characteristic of noisy, inconsiderate black people. West Indians lived mainly in multi-occupied houses and we soon discovered that any grouping of black people constituted a nuisance. White neighbours automatically complained about the noise. Often the police were called and they tended to deal with the situation in such a racist, uncivilised way that more problems were caused than solved. The way they barged right in was infuriating. They sometimes seized whatever drinks they found, on the pretext that drinks were being sold without a licence.

Everyone went to the cinema – very few people had television sets in the fifties. But most other forms of working class entertainment did not attract us. Brought up on a diet of American films, we could not appreciate the English humour of variety shows. Football, the dogs and horseracing were not really for us, largely because we had little spare cash. In addition to the high rents, our low wages had to cover the cost of sending money home for dependants or parents still there. Dances were popular with English people, but for West Indians they were like an obstacle course because of racism. First you had to get past the doorman. Then you had to be acceptably dressed to dance. And to get a partner, you had to get past the hurdle of the white men too. A night out at the Palais was fun only for the hardiest amongst us.

Eating out in restaurants was rare for any working class people, black or white. But it was a serious problem for us even to find acceptable food to take to work for lunches. Rice was our basic staple but often the only rice you could buy in the shops here was for puddings. Chicken was a luxury, which cut out another of our most familiar foods. Rabbit was comparatively cheap; when myxomatosis struck, it was a disaster for us, never mind the rabbits. Gradually, however, shopkeepers and street markets in areas where black people lived responded to demand and West Indian foodstuffs began to appear.

But a report in the Institute of Race Relations journal illustrated something of the kind of resistance we were up against. A Manchester butcher thought that, 'If West Indians want to eat goat meat they will have to go home to do it.' Another said, 'I wouldn't dream of getting it. It has a distinctive smell and might put customers off other kinds of meat.'[5] The few night clubs that were open to us were much too expensive and transport after eleven p.m. was a problem. Few of us owned cars. Those who did were fearful of the constant stopping and searching by the police. These pressures led to the establishment of our own 'alternative' clubs – 'blues' or 'basement' parties, where people were charged half a crown entry and another half a crown for drinks. This was illegal of course. And the parties did often cause a nuisance to neighbours, as they went on into the early hours. But they were inevitable, in the circumstances. As one man told me recently, 'The survival kit of black people is that we are experts on alternatives. It is an unconscious lesson of colonialism to find alternative ways of existing in a hostile environment, whether you're talking about food, school, culture or church.'

Against heavy odds, we certainly found alternative ways to survive socially. We didn't know then that the alternatives we were later to devise in the fields of education and working life would provide not only survival for ourselves, but the potential for change for all working people.

Notes

1. P. Fryer, *Staying Power: the history of black people in Britain*, Pluto, 1984.
2. Taken from *Eradicate Racism – a murderous crime*, a draft pamphlet by Tony Gilbert, Liberation, 1984.
3. Crowther Report, *15 to 18*, Central Advisory Council for Education (England), 1959.
4. B. Jackson and D. Marsden, *Education and the Working Class*, Routledge and Kegan Paul, 1962.
5. Institute of Race Relations Newsletter, January 1962.

3   Integration: a Hopeless Pursuit

I could never accept the idea of integration, because it centres on proving yourself to the white man.

We would take insults in the name of integration. We would read Shakespeare in the name of assimilation. The onus was on me: the less I demanded my rights, the more harmony there would be.

These statements, made with hindsight, represent illusions that were well shattered by the experience of the first ten to fifteen years of living in Britain. The irony is that West Indians came here by and large *assuming* integration – 'after all,' said one, 'it said on my passport that I *was* British.' Quickly realizing we had to fight for the equal rights and status which integration meant to us, we immigrant activists threw ourselves into promoting it. The government appeared also to support the notion of integration, or assimilation, but the period from 1950 to 1962 which roughly corresponds to the official pursuit of this social objective can now be seen as a time when the government employed divide-and-rule tactics, culminating in the first wave of anti-immigration laws and racist social policies, which slowly but surely undermined and subverted everybody's commitment to integration. It gradually became clear that there was an irreconcilable difference between the government's and the immigrants' views of integration. The former was about the absorption of black people into the 'norms' of white society, which would itself, of course, remain unruffled, unchanged and unchallenged. The latter was about participation based on equality.

Today, thirty-odd years later, black people in Britain are in many ways back to square one, arguing the case for race equality in social, political and economic terms. Current political reference points are a confusing mixture of racist laws, equality laws, Black Power, Rastafari and strategies ranging from separatism to aspiring to Parliament, the whitest bastion in the land. Today's generation of black activists might well believe that ours failed them. Where did our pursuit of integration get us? This chapter records the contribution of key groups of West Indian activists in the fifties and early sixties to the struggle for equality. The trade union and labour movement was the centre of our activity during this period; later on, as our children were born and grew older, the arena for black activism expanded, or even shifted, to the education system. Civil liberty and community rights issues have remained constant as priority issues, though in the early years these were included as often as not within the ambit of trade union activity rather than considered as separate spheres of involvement.

The international politics which defined our perspective were historically unique and it is important to understand that context if the role of our generation is to be properly understood. All of us ended up being disillusioned with the kind of integration that was on offer; some became disillusioned too with the organised left in British politics. What united many of us then, and continues to do so, is a commitment to socialism which is indivisible from the commitment to race equality. The experiences and perspectives we had are here to be reclaimed as part of the history not only of black people in this country but of the whole working class.

To the 'fifties generation' of the politically active West Indians, the vocabulary of alliances, unity and the broad left is not new. These things were the essence of our politics and practice. Unless they are genuinely recaptured and understood, by black people and white people alike, *our* definition of integration – participation on the basis of equality – will certainly be a hopeless pursuit.

We took it for granted that we would be on the left in Britain. Many of us joined the Communist Party or the Labour Party.

I was fascinated by all of it, from the beginning. I went to Woodford to hear Churchill speak and to Walthamstow to hear Attlee. I soon lost interest in Churchill, but didn't identify with anyone until I met Communists. Labour wasn't making sense. But when I heard Communists talk, things began to fall into place and I began to develop a sense of my own reality as a colonial person. It was the intellectual involvement which drew me into the CP, and the inspiration of the Russian revolution. Being in the party seemed natural to me and although I'm no longer a member I have never identified with anyone else since. There were Communists you admired all over the place, in every factory. They had a real strength.

I was met in London by three friends who were active politically and within their trade union. They were members of the Communist Party and it seemed natural to me that they were. We grew up in Trinidad during the Second World War when the Soviet Union was one of the Allied nations fighting against fascism, Nazism and racism. Coming from a colonial country, we were generally interested in and attracted by the heroic exploits of the Soviet Union. This was also the period when the struggle for national liberation was at its height. Britain was fighting six colonial wars. Agitation for independence was going on all over Africa, particularly in Ghana (then the Gold Coast), led by Kwame Nkrumah. The British Guianese elected government was deposed and the constitution abrogated. The political climate was hectic for many black workers and students. The solidarity of the British working class movement was at best ambivalent and at worst meaningless. The Cold War was rampant. The image of the United States was both anti-Communist and anti-black, with the McCarthy witch-hunts and the McCarren Walter Act restricting 'coloured' immigration. The French were fighting losing battles in Vietnam and Algeria. It seemed natural, therefore, for the Communist Party to be the home of black militants.

I came to England because my hopes for a political future in Jamaica were shattered. I had been a trade union leader and was imprisoned for my activities during a big strike in the sugar industry. When the witch-hunt within the PNP (Peoples' National Party) started, I was forced to leave. I came to England and applied to join the Communist Party after two weeks.

I was interested in politics and social justice as a child. Coming from the Caribbean, I could not have been a Conservative. When I came to Britain to train as a nurse, I joined the Labour Party. The post-war Labour government did not seem to be anti-black. It felt comfortable and gave me confidence. Through the West Indian Students' Union, I met all kinds of people from different political persuasions. Talking to them began to give me a heightened political awareness. My social life consisted of going to political meetings.

The Caribbean Labour Congress

Trade union membership in Britain had been rising fast ever since the end of the war. Black workers were at least as likely to join unions as white workers, if not more so. Many of us gained extensive trade union experience. Most active West Indian trade unionists in London also belonged to the Caribbean Labour Congress (London branch). The CLC was founded in 1945 as a coalition of political groupings mainly from the English-speaking West Indian islands. Its objectives were to fight for national liberation and to develop the concept of a Federation of West Indian islands which, it was thought, would enable the West Indies to be a more viable political and economic force in the world. The idea of a Federation was a controversial one and by the early sixties had been dropped. Some were suspicious that it was simply the brainchild of the Colonial Office, intended as a mechanism to ease the transition through independence and to provide a neo-colonialist apparatus afterwards. Others, particularly those of Indian origin, saw it as a way of consolidating the power of Afro-Caribbeans in sectarian opposition to the gains made by the Indo-Caribbean dominated Peoples' Progressive Party under Dr Cheddi Jagan in Guyana.

Nevertheless, the CLC commanded considerable influence to begin with in the West Indies. It was affiliated to the World Federation of Trade Unions, the body which linked trade unions from both the eastern and western European blocs. The Cold War, however, unleashed by Churchill's speech in Fulton, Missouri in 1946, led to the establishment of the competing body, the International Confederation of Trade Unions, by the USA with Britain's help. This undermined the influence of the CLC. Unions still affiliated to the WFTU were harassed by the colonial governments, aided and abetted by the British Parliament and the right-wing controlled Trades Union Congress. Trade union officials and activists were isolated, sacked and imprisoned. Leaders like Richard Hart, then an executive member of the Peoples' National Party of Jamaica were expelled from the Party. Many of those ostracised had to make the journey to Britain to find a political haven in the London Branch of the CLC, which kept up the organisation's work until the early sixties.

Although it was an organisation proscribed as a Communist front by the Labour Party and the TUC, it was nevertheless legal. The centre of its work was to provide political and financial support for the brothers and sisters carrying out the day-to-day struggle for national liberation in the West Indies. That support included developing solidarity within the labour, trade union and democratic movements in Britain. Despite its proscribed status, the CLC earned the respect of the labour movement as a 'fraternal organisation' and provided an important contact point between black and white activists. The London Trades Council sent a guest speaker to our sixth Annual General Meeting. Aneurin Bevan MP opened the West Indian Cultural Centre in London, formed jointly by the CLC and the League of Coloured People.

The CLC kept up our morale in the face of racism from all sides at the workplace, gave us political direction and enabled us to make a collective contribution to the labour movement as black workers. It was the CLC which was responsible for organising the presence of young black people at the World Youth Festivals, the first of which was in Yugoslavia in 1949. In my capacity as Youth Organiser for the CLC, I attended the Festival in Warsaw in 1955. As CLC members, we carried out hundreds of speaking engagements at trade union branches up and down the country, either drumming up support for the independence movement in the West Indies, or organising opposition to the first moves towards racist immigration laws in Britain. For example, as part of the campaign against these laws, the CLC wrote to all branches of the engineering workers' union, the AEU, in London, asking them to invite speakers to put the black case against. The response was overwhelming and illustrated the potential of an alliance on a specific issue between a militant, well informed black organisation whose members were all active trade unionists and a union under progressive leadership which genuinely wanted to see its membership properly informed and educated on a broad range of issues which had implications for the whole movement.

The CLC's paper, *Caribbean News*, was published in London, monthly then bi-monthly, from November 1952 until June 1956. It was the first black political journal in Britain since the war. It was succeeded in 1958 by the *West Indian Gazette*, edited by the Communist Claudia Jones, who continued the socialist and internationalist perspective which *Caribbean News* had promoted, but also focused more on social and cultural issues relevant to the West Indian community in Britain and, in particular, used the paper as a campaigning weapon against the developing anti-immigration lobby. The *West Indian Gazette* continued until Claudia Jones's death in 1964.[1]

During its relatively short life, *Caribbean News* fulfilled an important role for West Indian activists both in Britain and in the Caribbean. It was banned as subversive material in most West Indian islands, much to the delight of the editorial team in London, who considered a ban by such anti-progressive forces to be a compliment to their political views. Despite the ban, ways and means were found of getting the paper through to our comrades at home.

The essential internationalism of our political framework included solidarity work in support of the various African national liberation struggles, particularly in Kenya. But even nearer to home and closer to the West Indian heart was the inspiration of the victory of the Cuban revolution in 1959. Although the imperialist master was the United States, the similarities were very clear. Cuba was very similar in its economic structure and cosmopolitan population to Jamaica,

Trinidad and Guyana. Although independent on paper, Cuba's economic and political relationship to the United States did not differ very much from that of the British West Indian colonies to Britain. The triumph in Cuba and the outcome of the African struggles, therefore, struck a chord of defiance and a vision of hope for the future in the minds of black people in Britain. A little later, as I shall describe in the next chapter, the influence of Black Power from the United States captured the hearts and minds of the black community to an even more significant extent.

Looking back at the editions of *Caribbean News*, a picture emerges of Britain which is not only the untold story of the black trade unionists of the time, but is also an insight into that part of the whole trade union and labour movement which had contact with us. It shows that there were pockets within the movement which, thanks to the combination of enlightened leadership and the influence of a black perspective, had broadened its view of its own role and interests away from the narrow 'bread-and-butter' outlook which has tended to dominate over most of the past thirty years.

Over and over again, *Caribbean News* hammered home its main messages to West Indian workers in Britain: join your trade union and work for unity between black and white people. There are dozens of reports of trade union branches and trades councils holding meetings with a CLC speaker. Discussion often centred around the connections between Britain's 'colour bar', colonialism and big business. Meeting after meeting passed resolutions of solidarity and called on government, employers and workers alike to take action to stop race discrimination. The paper carried the kinds of stories it would not have been possible to read elsewhere, except possibly in the *Daily Worker*, since they gave the lie to the myths of the mass media which pitted worker against worker, using race as a very convenient tool. In *Caribbean News* we read of the CLC's support for the successful dockers' strike in 1954:

> For 28 days the port workers of Britain have been on strike, in the biggest stoppage in British labour history since the General Strike in 1926. This militant action by the dockers in defence of their

elementary rights has ended in victory for them. Their strike was no picnic as some tend to think, but involved severe sacrifice by the men, their wives and children. The Caribbean Labour Congress (London Branch) was privileged to make a contribution of £2 to the strike fund, and in this small way to show the solidarity of West Indian workers with their British comrades.

We must have all remembered our support for this dockers' strike fourteen years later and wondered whatever happened to solidarity: in 1968 the dockers were amongst those who rallied and demonstrated their support for Enoch Powell when he made his 'rivers of blood' speech, which even some establishment Tories found difficult to swallow.

Other stories in *Caribbean News* demonstrate two-way solidarity in action between black and white workers. Under the headline 'Black and White Together' in the October 1955 edition, we read of the month-long strike at the Ann Shelley clothing factory in Stepney, East London. 125 workers, of whom twenty were black, had walked out in protest against management behaviour:

They are refusing to work subject to the abuse, insults and vile language from a floor manager. One time previously, as a result of complaints against this man and a stoppage, the management removed him from his position. But he has been reinstated and has once more returned to his old ways.

The firm now refuses to do anything about it, or to negotiate with the trade union to end the dispute ...

This strike is demonstrating in action the unity of the workers, black and white, of English, West Indian, and Pakistani men and women ... Mr H. Regal, factory convenor, told me, '... it's really remarkable to see coloured women earning £5 or £6 a week and having to pay around £2 5s a week for a single furnished room, paying bus fares and coming across London regularly to stand in the picket line.' Mr Regal has been in the trade union movement for 31 years and he should know.

I spoke to three Jamaican girls this morning on the picket line outside the factory in Commercial Road ... the girls would rather not have their names in print, but one young woman who had worked for Ann Shelley for two years showed keenness in putting up a fight. The incident occurred in another shop but she also came out in sympathy ... Their English mates on the picket line were full of praise for the West Indian girls' tenacity in this long, bitter struggle.

The management is trying to get strikebreakers from outside the factory, and their shop windows are stuck up with advertisements of vacancies. Few outsiders have stepped across the picket lines, however. The management made an attempt to split the workers when they sent a telegram to a coloured woman asking her to get her friends to come in, but without success.

They also held back the coloured workers' pay packets when the white workers had already been paid off ... These efforts to split the workers have led to nought, for the unity displayed on the picket lines between black and white is teaching an important lesson for the whole working class. A leaflet issued by the strikers says:

'The firm seems determined to break the spirit of the workers, but they will not succeed. We fight for a principle. The principle that no manager shall speak to workers as though we were living in the middle ages. We fight for the right of the workers to have self-respect. We fight to teach the management that 125 workers are worth more to them than an insulting manager.'

Other articles show how some unions were prepared to intervene directly to avert racist practices against their black members from white members. In the spring of 1956, for example, NUR officials stopped an overtime ban in Haringey by workers opposed to the employment of a Jamaican shunter. For two years the workers had been fighting against the recruitment of any 'coloured or foreign' shunters. Following a meeting with an official who reminded the men of national union policy, normal working was resumed.

Fears over job security could lead to a confusion between racial discrimination (or the 'colour bar') and policies to bar foreign labour. The distinction was made on one occasion by the National Union of Mineworkers, following press reports that a Jamaican miner had been refused a job at the Denaby Colliery by a Labour Officer who claimed that 'the white coal miners would not work with a coloured man'. The CLC wrote to the secretary of the Denaby NUM, who replied:

The first intimation we had that this man had even sought employment at this colliery was when we saw the statement in the *Daily Herald* that we had refused to work with Fabion McIntosh because he was coloured. These are the facts. In 1950 this branch along with every other miners' branch in the country was asked if we would accept foreign labour in our pits. This labour was Italian and Polish and we, like many other branches in South Yorkshire, refused; our reason for refusing being (a) we were of the opinion that the mining industry could be made attractive enough to attract British labour, and (b) we had a fairly large number of young miners who were waiting to be upgraded and in our opinion the introduction of foreign labour would make their position worse.

We never at any time discussed the problem from the point of view of the man's colour. In fact, a coloured Jamaican worked at this pit for many years until he died. His two sons commenced as boys, one worked here until he died some 12 months ago, and the other is still working happily alongside us.

[The Labour Officer], without even consulting the branch to see if his facts were correct, told [Mr McIntosh] he could not come to Denaby as the branch would not work with coloured or foreign nationals, thus imputing that we at Denaby were operating the colour bar. We strongly resent this and say quite bluntly that we do not mind whatever colour a man is, if he is a worker and a trade union member he will be treated with the same consideration by us as any other worker.

The role of the popular press in whipping up race hatred, distorting the amount of support for the colour bar and misrepresenting union action is exposed in a number of stories covered in *Caribbean News*. One of these was about a meeting of Transport and General Workers' Union members in London, comprising oil company workers and Stockwell Bus Garage representatives. The members expressed their anger at inaccurate press reports about a dispute in which the bus workers were protesting about lack of management consultation, but which had been publicised as worker opposition to black recruits. The bus workers had been unsuccessful in getting factual corrections printed in the press. The meeting dismissed the idea that 'coloured workers' were a danger to trade unions or could be used to break a strike. A unanimous resolution was passed recognising 'the common struggle of the British working class and the colonial workers coming into this country' and calling for 'unity in the fight for freedom of all colonial peoples'.

The reports and stories in *Caribbean News*, however, probably represent the sum total of anti-racism within the labour movement at the time. The daily grind most of us faced was the reality of racism wherever we looked. For in general, alongside our battles against the employer, black people have always also had to fight to gain recognition of their existence in and contribution to the labour movement. In the same way as women have been invisible as trade unionists, because sexism prevents the traditional image of a trade unionist from being anything but that of a male, white manual worker, so black people have had to struggle to be visible through the fog of racism. We found it very difficult in the fifties to understand white workers' lack of sympathy towards our particular problems as immigrant workers. The dominant view of the role of trade unions by their membership seemed to be very narrow. Wages and conditions was one thing, but the politics of colonialism was quite another, especially if your own personal attitudes and feelings were implicated. Indeed, it took us a while to understand that white workers did not tend even to socialise with each other in the same way as we traditionally did. We expected the fact of trade union membership and the spirit of workplace solidarity to consist of more than the infrequent branch meeting.

Ironically, the more tightly organised the industry or workplace, the more difficult it was for black people to get work, despite virtuous statements from national union leaderships about equality and working class solidarity. It was, and still is, nearly impossible for black people to become printers. Word-of-mouth recruitment, which effectively restricts access to employment within certain families ('Dads' Lads') and small communities, was even more prevalent in the large wholesale markets like Covent Garden. This and similar practices also discriminated against many white workers but it seemed to go on unquestioned and tolerated by them. Black trade unionists could not understand or sympathise with the tradition; they saw simply that an organisation in which they had placed their trust, and which they expected to defend them, operated as viciously against their interests as did the bosses.

The requirement to have completed an apprenticeship also barred black workers from many craft industries, where a colour bar was practised. Sometimes access to an apprenticeship was only possible if the young worker already had relatives in the industry. It was virtually impossible to get a job in the print industry without a union card. But of course it was a vicious circle, as the union card could only be obtained if you had a job. Ways did emerge to break through such barriers. A trade in counterfeit apprenticeship certificates grew. So perfect were the fake certificates (they were dipped in tea to look old) that both employers and union officials were fooled.

The following three acounts from black trade unionists reflect some of the different and conflicting experiences which faced black people on the left in the fifties:

I became the AEU shop steward on the night shift at the Frigidaire factory, after being there a year. I had been one of the strike leaders during the first stoppage in the factory, which lasted five and a half weeks. When I became shop steward, they wanted to transfer me. I tried to resist but they threatened to bring in the police, so I reluctantly agreed to move. Three hours later, I was told that the men had walked out and would stay out until I was put back. I immediately joined them. The personnel manager sent for me and we negotiated a compromise: I could return after a week. A few weeks later, we had a big strike over piece work. I discovered peoples' trust in me.

I had a job on a building site several miles outside London, where 90 per cent of the workforce was Irish. Within three days we had made friends. There was no union, but after five days I called a meeting to discuss the organisation of the site. We organised one section of the workforce and I was elected shop steward. But as most of the workers were not permanent, the firm didn't worry too much as they thought it couldn't last. We got them to make some important improvements though, like a decent canteen and a first aid centre.

Then one day, a worker was sacked for lateness. It was unfair, because he had been ill but had no access to a doctor. We threatened to strike if he wasn't reinstated. The firm's response to that was to threaten *me* with dismissal! Throughout the whole dispute, none of the English workers on the site got involved or showed any commitment to the union at all. But they must have been giving messages to the handful of other black workers, though, because one day the other black labourers put it to me that my trade union activity 'was making it bad for them'. By that time, I had been in the job for seven months and was feeling cut off from politics in London. So I resigned. For the following twelve years I worked in London and almost everywhere was elected shop steward.

I would say that I have never experienced any personal racism from fellow union officials. On two occasions I experienced racism from other workers. In one case, where I was the shop steward and the only black in the workforce, some of the men complained that they didn't want to be represented by a black man. But my supporters argued for me on the basis of my experience. The other time, I was opposed by Irish Catholics for being a Communist. It was the time of Kennedy's assassination. So as shop steward I closed down the factory for the day in his memory. The Irish workers instantly changed their attitude to me. The management dismissed me a week later, but the men said they would all walk out in sympathy – they were prepared to have the site close permanently rather than see me dismissed. I was reinstated.

Working with the trade union movement has been my best enjoyment in England. It gave me the same feeling as going home to a happy family.

I had joined the Caribbean Labour Congress soon after I arrived in Britain. Realising that improved working conditions depended on the strength of shopfloor organisation – and that, more generally, improvements in the quality of life and living standards demanded collective action – I joined the Union of Shop, Distributive and Allied Workers. The factory, Wiseman's, was not unionised at all at the time, but within a couple of weeks I had recruited ten fellow workers, a sixth of the workforce. They were

Turkish, Maltese and two young English lads. The management took a dim view of my activities and union membership was strongly discouraged. One strategy was to offer a small increase on the basic wage to anyone thought to be tempted by the union. I had first-hand experience of another management tactic: I was invited to the manager's office one day. I assumed I was going to be hauled over the coals for my union activities, but to my surprise I was complimented on my intelligence and my work. I was puzzled until he suggested to me that I should go to the nearest Labour Exchange and recruit black people for shopfloor jobs with the firm. My response was blunt and to the point. No way was I going to encourage anybody to work under those foul conditions. Without any visible rancour, the idea was dropped.

When I was elected shop steward in USDAW, it was made clear to me by workmates that their trust in me was despite being a Communist, rather than despite being black. 'We know that reds never rat,' they told me, 'but don't think we would ever elect you to Parliament or the council.' But although being black was apparently no obstruction to my becoming shop steward, I did find it difficult to participate in the trade union movement and in my branch meetings as an equal. No one seemed to listen to or believe our complaints about racism, whether within the union, or outside, such as with housing problems or general abuse in the streets. Trade unions were simply not constructed with black people in mind. As a result of pressure from the few black members, the London organisation of USDAW did try, in the mid-fifties, to devise ways of attracting and involving black people. But this work was difficult to develop, as black people tended to stay for such short periods in their bad, low-paid jobs – usually just six months to a year. As a consequence, those of us who were politically conscious and active would give priority to our international solidarity work. As far as domestic and internal union issues were concerned, the dogma of class-before-race presented a barrier we could not penetrate; indeed, part of the problem was that we fell for it ourselves.

Race and Class

The relegation and neglect of race issues was a problem inside the political parties of the working class as well as in the trade union movement. In the Communist Party at least, the

problem was partially acknowledged and partially addressed
for a time. In the light of the debate and controversy in the
eighties about black sections in the Labour Party, a look back
at how the issue was articulated in the fifties can perhaps
provide some pointers towards a more satisfactory solution in
today's political climate.

In London there was a thriving West Indian branch of the
Communist Party in the early fifties, which had been set up in
response to the difficulties faced by many black members in
working within the ordinary party framework. Their
complaints were similar to those of the black trade unionists.
First, issues which most concerned them appeared irrelevant to
the average British party member; secondly, there were the
racist and colonialist attitudes that ran through the veins of
most white people, Communists included. The West Indian
comrades recognised nevertheless the important role played by
the party, both nationally and internationally. Some felt that
their participation would be made easier by forming a caucus
which could inform the party on questions that would not
otherwise receive proper attention. This was not a unanimous
position. Some felt that a separate branch or caucus would
cause dissent and confusion and, in any case, would not
necessarily promote the political development of the ordinary
white party member.

There were also West African and Cypriot Party branches in
London. The West Indian branch was about fifty members
strong in the fifties. Many of the West Indians were students,
who had joined the party for social as well as political reasons.
Those in work were encouraged to join their workplace branch
too. There was also a West Indian advisory committee of the
party, at national level. Two members from this advisory body
sat on the International Committee; they were invited to
participate in Executive Committee discussions relating to
racism or to solidarity work on the various independence
struggles. Three or four times a year, an aggregate meeting was
held for all West Indian comrades. About a hundred and fifty
would attend. The deficiency of this model was that black
comrades were not sufficiently integrated into other areas of

political work, for example through the industrial or political committees.

The existence of the West Indian, West African and Cypriot branches was peculiar to London. They were not part of a national policy strategy within the party; indeed, the party opposed the pressure to set up a similar West African branch in Liverpool. Had there been a proper analysis at the time, which recognised that racial oppression cannot just be neatly packaged up in subordination to class oppression, then the West Indian branch might have survived and the allegiance of those comrades preserved. As it was, the branch gradually petered out by about 1956, as the work of the West Indian advisory (which included white Communists) took over. The vast majority of the party's black members left over the following decade. This exodus was later mirrored by the loss of large numbers of Cypriots when their branch was abolished in favour of integration into the 'mainstream' branches.

Other major influences were also behind the departure of the black membership of the party during that period. By the early sixties most of the former colonial countries had achieved independence and it had been the drive of the movement for independence, rather than a specifically socialist commitment, which had drawn in many of the activists in the first place. Many people misunderstood what political independence mean for colonial countries. The achievement of national independence filled many comrades with a sense of dignity which suggested their struggle was complete. But the politics of a national liberation struggle did not make that struggle an automatic precursor of a society based on equality. An alliance of different social forces, with different interests and ideologies, could win independence. But within that alliance were three main strands. First, the bourgeois national democrats, whose main objective was to replace the white representatives of imperialism with themselves. They negotiated terms of independence which did not necessarily constitute a break with what we subsequently described as neo-colonialism. Secondly, there were the cultural nationalists, whose main desire was to destroy imperialist cultural dominance, but who did not necessarily attack the fundamental political and economic structures of the society. Thirdly, there was the socialist component, which recognised that the struggle for independence was only the beginning of the struggle for true liberation and equality.

A number of black members of the Communist Party in the fifties were students who had come to Britain from very poor and disadvantaged backgrounds. After gaining some kind of professional qualification, they faced a bitter dilemma. They could either return home and fill the gaps left by the white agents of imperialism, which meant breaking with the left and socialism; or they could continue with the struggle, which meant they faced a lifetime of swimming against the stream, consigned to the margins of society. Those not rooted in socialist commitment tended to opt for the former path and were lost to the left and the labour movement.

Others, who did hold deep socialist convictions, left the Communist Party though they remained in Britain. Ironically, the achievement of a socialist revolution in Cuba in 1959 was one of the influences behind this move. It appeared on the surface that Fidel Castro and his supporters had pulled off the revolution without the need for a Communist Party. It was not until two years after the revolution that Castro re-organised, joined and led Cuba's Communist Party. Only later did it become clear that however successful and charismatic Fidel and co. were in leading the revolution from the mountains, it could not have been safeguarded and consolidated without the party's work on the ground at the same time. In 1959, however, the impact of the revolution on politically active West Indians in Britain led to a certain distancing from the Party here.

The other influence at an international level which affected black membership of the party was Khrushchev's speech to the 20th Congress of the CPSU in 1956, where the political crimes of Stalin were announced and denounced. The shock of these revelations to all comrades, black and white, was, of course, a serious watershed in the history of the Party. Their impact on West Indian immigrants in Britain, however, was significant in a specific way. Many of those who were in the party at the time say that it was not so much the British party they felt they had joined, but rather the international Communist movement. Even today, some ex-party members still describe themselves as Communists whatever the reason they left the party. The Soviet Union was at the heart of that international movement and had been seen to play a key role in the anti-colonialist and anti-imperialist struggles of which the black Communists in Britain were a product and a part. The denunciation of Stalin came as a severe emotional shock. It seemed that Marxism had failed or was failing. At the same time, the crimes perpetrated by Stalin, when interpreted from a political perspective which has grown out of slavery, with all the humiliation, death and torture that entailed, did not seem quite so staggeringly offensive as they must have done to white people whose political heritage is centred on democracy.

Racism within the Communist Party, both at the theoretical level and in practical and personal terms, added its weight to the growing disillusionment of many of the black comrades in the fifties and sixties. The party's programme, *The British Road to Socialism* (1951 version) reflected the colonialist assumptions of the ruling class in the way it envisaged the relationship between a future socialist Britain and future socialist countries in the West Indies and elsewhere in the Commonwealth. The assumption was that there would be a 'fraternal association' between these countries, with the West Indian socialist countries looking to a socialist Britain in much the same way as they had been conditioned to look to Britain as the 'motherland' in colonial days. Black comrades took this up in the party, arguing that it was arrogant of the Party leadership to assume such a colonialist position and pointing out that, were the West Indies and Britain ever to be socialist, then of course there would be fraternal *relations*, but that the West Indian countries would be autonomous and almost certainly likely to look elsewhere for the more organised and politically logical kind of relationship which a 'fraternal association' implies. A Central or South American country which had become socialist would have far greater real links with a socialist West Indies than would Britain on the basis of being our ex-colonial master. The black comrades who challenged the party leadership on this question, however, got nowhere until 1957, when the formulation was changed at a special congress at which R. Palme Dutt's argument carried the day. Sadly, however, many of Dutt's West Indian comrades had not been prepared to wait for 1957 and had left the party.

Inefficient procedures for dealing with membership, or racism, or a combination of the two, led to other black comrades drifting out of the Communist Party, even when they had no fundamental disagreement with its policies. One, who had not even supported the existence of the West Indian Branch because he believed it to be a diversion from the main class struggle, decided when he became a law student to cut down on active politics:

> I went to the branch secretary and explained, saying that I wanted to keep paying my dues anyway. After a while, nobody was there to pay my dues to, so eventually I stopped. No one sought me out. So I just lapsed.

Another, who is still a party member today, recalls how difficult he found it to join the party in the first place, despite being a prominent local leader in tenants' organisations, community politics and his local trade union branch:

> I had represented the black workers at a branch of my union where the secretary was a party member. I was looking for a CP branch to join, but no one tried to recruit me or point me in the right direction. I finally filled in a form, but heard nothing for three months. There had been other Communists involved in the rent strikes I had helped to organise, but none of them introduced themselves as such to me. Two years later I was the chair of my local party branch and ended up standing twice for election as a local councillor for the party.

At one stage, a group of black comrades went on a delegation to the party's General Secretary to complain about the racism in the party which effectively denied them access to leadership positions. No black person was on the Executive

Committee at the time. They had been told they were 'on the periphery of development' and needed more time and experience in the movement. The people rightly offended by this insult included comrades who had come to this country after being imprisoned in the West Indies for leading national strikes as part of the anti-colonialist struggle, who had thrown themselves into the work of the trade union and labour movement as soon as they had arrived in Britain and who had practised their politics wherever they found themselves – at work and in their communities – in a way which the party only many years later was to develop as a theory of political practice called 'the broad democratic alliance'.

The lack of understanding on the part of white party leaders, shared by the leadership of the left and labour movement in general, of the colonial background of black activists filled us with a deep sense of frustration.

> One of the things militating against black people is that the left has always seen us on the periphery of political development. Even those of us who have been around a long time. Most of us who came here had a political background, but colonialism has left a deep mark on how Europeans see us. In the colonial setting, black people are always seen as the second tier of anything. Always the sergeants, never the lieutenants or generals. This was even the case in the MCF [Movement for Colonial Freedom] where so many of us were active. It was controlled by white activists, with very few black people in the leadership. Respect is a different thing from being given the opportunity to give leadership. The left is always showing respect – and they make you an outreach worker! That is at the root of black peoples' frustration with the organised working class movement – that lip service, that denial of our potential. They have double standards in their expectations.

Yet the comrade whose words are quoted above has remained in the party. Many of us who got frustrated and grumbled were sustained in our political faith by the encouragement of Claudia Jones. 'Struggle begets struggle,' she would say. We also remembered that, despite our feelings of being the dispossessed underclass in the working class

struggle, our achievement of liberation and equality could not
be won in a vacuum.

> I stayed in the Communist Party because I disagreed with those
> who claimed that the racism of the left was an inherent and
> permanent feature of their attitudes. I felt that since racism was
> part of the ideological structure of a bourgeois capitalist society,
> those same comrades could learn and change their attitudes. An
> important feature in my thinking was that in order to liberate
> myself and other black people, we have also got to help liberate
> our white brothers and sisters. You can't win one struggle without
> the other. But what convinced me more than anything was seeing
> how the many black comrades who left the party found themselves
> in what I would describe as a rudderless ship, and how quickly
> careerism became of paramount importance in their lives.
>
> I was one of those who went to complain to Johnny Gollan
> [General Secretary of the Communist Party from 1956 to 1974]
> about the lack of black leadership in the party. But I have stuck
> with it. That was the only serious disagreement I've had with the
> party in all these years. I don't think the Party is dealing properly
> with racism and sometimes I get angry. But I know who I am. I am
> a Communist and I have come to terms with where I can and can't
> reach. I have a sense of fulfilment being a Communist and I'm not
> selling out. The Labour Party occasionally has enticed me, but I
> know that my political education couldn't improve anywhere but
> in the Communist Party.

In spite of the handful of faithful survivors, it cannot be
denied that the stubborn class-before-race position of the
party during the fifties and sixties cost the party dearly in terms
of its members. Towards the end of the sixties, as we shall see
in the next chapter, came the impact of Black Power, which
captured and reactivated many of the disaffected activists.
Black Power had powerful and positive features, but it
dampened the spirit of class struggle in the minds of many
black people, replacing it with the obsverse of the class-
before-race ideology which had frustrated them. Suddenly race
became the primary issue and the organized left, which had no
satisfactory answer to this proposition, was abandoned in large

numbers by black activists. This loss has never been acknowledged by the left in general or the Communist Party in particular. Everyone knows of the exodus after Hungary in 1956 and after Czechoslovakia in 1968, but the disaffection of significant numbers of black comrades, although it took place more gradually than that which affected people around the events of 1956 or 1968, did not seem to register as a milestone of the same importance or magnitude in the history of the party.

Rejection by the white organisations of the left, combined with isolation from natural community support and the desire to combat racism, led to the formation of numerous black organisations of a political or cultural nature. The Caribbean Labour Congress has already been referred to, as the haven for the most politically conscious amongst us. Other organisations were social rather than political, although the dividing line is difficult to draw.

> I was in a local community organisation which had been set up to provide solidarity for black people. I didn't see it as political, more social. We played dominoes, talked about home, discussed our common problems over housing. We would go and meet new arrivals at Paddington Station.

The Black Community

Dozens of small organisations sprang up based on the island loyalty of those who had come here from various parts of the West Indies. Groups like the Trinidad and Tobago Association and similar organisations for people from Jamaica, Guyana, Dominica and Monserrat all attracted their members and most still exist today, affiliated to the umbrella organisation, the West Indian Standing Conference (WISC) which was founded in 1958 and is still active. The longest established organisation in the fifties was the League of Coloured People, founded in 1931 by Dr Moody. The League was modelled on the National Association for the Advancement of Colored People in the USA and attracted mainly students and middle class groups. Although anti-racist, the League was philanthropic in its approach and concentrated on social activities for black people. This played an important role in the days when so many clubs, pubs and hotels operated the colour bar. Our campaigns against this type of discrimination got a boost in 1954 when Learie Constantine's book *Colour Bar* was published.[2] The world-famous cricketer, who was later to be knighted, told the story of how he was refused service in 1944 by Imperial London Hotels, when he was a welfare officer in the RAF. He took legal action against the hotel which had discriminated against him and won nominal damages. But it was still to be many years before we had the law positively on our side against such discrimination, as opposed to a situation where only individuals determined to take on the courts single-handed could hope to find a remedy. The West Indian businessman who was fined for driving without insurance in 1961, for example, could do nothing about the discrimination which had led him to commit an offence. He had approached fifteen companies for van insurance and all had returned his money when they discovered he was black. The British Insurance Association denied discrimination, but an individual broker said he knew at least 180 companies which banned insurance being issued to black customers, or offered discriminatory terms, such as a three-year residence rule, or a premium 25 per cent higher than usual, on the grounds that West Indians were temperamentally a worse risk than other drivers.

The late fifties and early sixties saw us all shedding the last vestiges of the illusion that we were in any way equal citizens of the United Kingdom. If white people spoke to us in a civil manner in the streets, there was always a sting in the tail. 'When did you arrive?' they would ask first, followed up quickly by the second question, 'When are you going back?' We, who had been brought up on English history and literature, had to come to terms with the blanket ignorance of the English themselves of the whereabouts of the West Indies, never mind our history and culture. A typical response to discovering that a workmate came from Trinidad, for example, was, 'Oh, that's just north of Nigeria, isn't it?'

The ignorance and hostility of white people motivated us into forming black or island groups, whether for social contact and comfort or to organise and articulate our views as part of an organisation such as a trade union which seemed pathologically incapable of representing our interests.

I got involved with my union at the Paddington telephone exchange. The workforce was 90 per cent black and the white shop stewards didn't care about us. We had a meeting of black workers and they elected me as spokesperson. There was no way the shop steward would deal with me on that basis – we were just told that we simply could not organise in that fashion. But at the AGM of the branch I stood as shop steward and won.

Trinidadians at Carnival time (which falls just before Lent) were a particularly sorry sight. When we first came to this country, many of us just didn't go into work for the two days we would have been celebrating at home. The Carnival spirit was so deeply ingrained that we felt we were missing out on a serious and important occasion. The vacuum we felt was made worse by the grimness and aggression of the British environment. One of the first initiatives taken by Claudia Jones after she came to London following her deportation from the United States for her Communist activity was to stage the first Carnival dance. Hundreds of us came together at St Pancras Town Hall and the event was even televised by the BBC. A couple of years later, probably 1960, four well known Trinidadian musicians toured the streets of Ladbroke Grove in West London on a truck with a steel band. They were joining in a long-established English carnival tradition which was celebrated in that area already. Carnival with a West Indian flavour had taken root. Every year after that more and more bands joined in, people started following the trucks and using costumes. Later on, the Carnival Development Committee was set up and the event grew into the largest street festival in Europe. Its political and social significance is described further in the next chapter.

In the same year as Claudia Jones set the Carnival ball rolling, a milestone of a different kind sent shock waves throughout the country. The racist violence which erupted in 1958 and 1959 in Notting Hill in London and in Nottingham marked a terrifying shift in the way we felt we were seen by white people. It also changed the way we saw ourselves. We had been used to the everyday verbal abuse in the streets, in shops, factories and on the buses; teddy boys used to pick fights, but we did not fear for our lives or think that our houses could be burned down. But the murder of Kelso Cochrane by a gang of six white youths in Notting Hill in 1959 signalled something new on the scene. There had been witnesses to the murder but the culprits were never found.

Rumour has it that the 1958 riots were sparked off when a white woman was called a 'black man's trollop' by white men in a pub. An incident like this may well have been a contributory factor, or the last straw against the background of a range of social and economic tensions which led to the riots. White male racism was pushed to the brink by the 'insult' of white women choosing to go out with black men. Not only had we come to take their jobs, they figured illogically, but their women too. The racism and sexism of white men converged in their abhorrence of both the notion that black men were 'defiling' the 'purity' of white women and also of the idea that white women were expressing sexual independence.

> 1958 was the watershed for me. Something much more deep and poisonous began to divide people.

The West Indian community now lived in fear of indiscriminate attack. Many women never walked in the street at night again. Property as well as people came under attack. And slogans like KBW (Keep Britain White) were daubed on walls by organised extreme right-wing groups.

The background to all this, in the eyes of the politicians, the media and ordinary white people, was of course the exaggerated and fabricated fear of never-ending immigration, which was manipulated to nurture racism. Writers in the gutter press fulminated against 'spongers' from the West Indies. 'Thousands just want to come and loaf – to sit on your back and mine and cash in on National Assistance, the health scheme and all the services of the Welfare State,' was a typical offering from the *Sunday People*. The 1958 racist riots strengthened the lobby for immigration restrictions and deportation. But, as Tom Driberg MP pointed out to the 1958 Trades Union Congress, we were only 190,000 out of over 50 million and 'the real problem is not black skins, but white prejudice.' The immigration figures for the fifties bear this out plainly. By 1958, 125,000 West Indians had arrived since the end of the war. During the fifties, immigrants from India and Pakistan also began to arrive in significant numbers, 55,000 by 1958. All these people also possessed British citizenship and the right of permanent residence. The really telling figures, though, are the ones which show the relative size of black immigration compared to white. For example, as *Caribbean News* reported in July 1955, Board of Trade figures for the first six months of that year revealed that together with 3,600 West Indian immigrants, 3,200 Canadians and 6,700 Australians also came to settle in Britain.

> The attention of the press to the government has, however, been almost entirely concentrated upon the West Indian immigrants, in a way calculated to stir up racial prejudice. We believe that if the facts were presented to the people of Britain in their proper proportion, it would be seen that to talk of restriction was to react hysterically to a situation which poses no serious problems.

The Asian communities in Britain were more heavily mobilised in fighting the plans to introduce restrictions to immigration than we were, although Claudia Jones with her campaigning *West Indian Gazette* and tireless work with the Afro-Asian-Caribbean Conference played an important role in fostering unity and growth amongst the anti-racist lobbies against the restrictions, both at the Parliamentary and local community levels. By 1962, however, when the Commonwealth Immigration Bill became law, most West Indians who were coming to Britain were already here. The Asians, on the other hand, were much more severely trapped by the voucher system which the Act introduced, suffering acute separation

within families and with no other country but Britain to turn
to.

Claudia Jones's political background and experience gave
her an understanding of the implications of the new law which
was deeper and more sophisticated than that of most other
West Indians in Britain. She had been in the States when the
McCarren Walter Act 1952 was passed (which restricted black
immigration) and understood immediately the historical and
political significance of the Act we were now facing in Britain.
Without her inspiration and leadership, we might have allowed
the relative lack of personal threat posed by the Act to our
status and our families (compared to its impact on the Asian
communities) to inhibit our opposition. We recognised
personal racism against us, sure enough, as the insults on the
streets and the hostility of the media escalated. But Claudia
encouraged us to analyse the role of the Act in terms of
structural racism within society at large: institutional racism, as
we later came to call it. Claudia's vision made this issue clear
for her. Thrust into the thick of London politics from the
United States and bringing with her a famous political
reputation, she was seen as a working class intellectual,
different and 'American', but someone with whom everyone
felt they could identify. She could deal with any level of society.
Although she was a well known Communist, everyone wanted
to speak to her and read what she had written. She challenged
our sectarianism. Her attitude and analysis of racism was
something new to us. She would rekindle the conscience in
those of us who were tempted to feel comfortable; she would
inspire and befriend the ones who felt despondent and lonely.
Her professional accomplishments matched her personal
skills. As a trained journalist, she was able to get the message
across through the *West Indian Gazette* in a way which
commanded a much broader appeal than its predecessor,
Caribbean News. When the Commonwealth Immigration Act
became law in February 1962, it did not occur to her to accept
defeat: she was one of the leaders responsible for organising a
mass demonstration with a strong West Indian presence,
including many black nurses in uniform.

Claudia's gift to the black community was her political analysis as well as her sterling campaigning work. In one of her last pieces of writing, in 1964, for an American Communist Party journal, she connects the economic rationale with the racist motivation behind the 1962 Act in Britain and the subsequent sell-out of the Labour Party, which had opposed the Bill when it was introduced by a Tory government, but later made a 'gentleman's agreement' with the government over its renewal.[3] The straightforward economic explanation of the Act was, of course, that Britain's labour requirements were no longer the same as they had been immediately after the war, when the shortage had been so acute that the government recruited directly from the West Indies. Britain was now engaged in unsuccessful attempts to join the Common Market and had to be seen as a potential workplace for Europeans, not ex-colonials. Domestically too, the 'reserve army of labour' had changed character, from black men to white women. When the West Indian workforce was recruited after the war, British women were being told to stay at home and be good wives and mothers. But between 1951 and 1971 the labour force grew by 2.5 million people, of whom 2.3 million were women. The growth of the service industries and the public sector provided employment for women, who to a significant extent replaced immigrant labour as the material seen fit to plug the projected 'manpower gap'. (Not insignificantly, yet another 'gentleman's agreement', this time between the Labour government and the TUC, put the lid on the pressure for equal pay for women throughout this period. Institutional sexism and institutional racism worked in harmony to maintain divide-and-rule within the working class.) But even if the twin trends of female entry into the labour market and of continuing immigration were consciously seen to be conflicting ones, the simplest statistics could put paid to such a theory. As Claudia Jones pointed out:

> All Tory claims that the Act would benefit either Britain or the immigrants are, of course, easily refuted. The most widely prevalent Tory argument was that coloured immigrants were

'flooding Britain'. At the time of the Act's passage, the 1961 British population census showed a two and a half million increase, during the very period of the growth of the immigration of West Indians and Afro-Asians, and this increase was easily absorbed by the British economy. The coloured migrant is less than one in every hundred people. Yearly emigration of Britons shows that for every single person entering Britain, *three* leave its shores.

The shibboleth that 'immigrants take away houses and jobs', when viewed in the light of Tory responsibility for high interest property rates and the Rent Act makes this claim likewise ludicrous. As for new houses, there is no evidence that West Indians or other coloured immigrants have taken away any houses. Allowed largely to purchase old, dilapidated, short-lease houses, it is the West Indian building worker, who helps to construct new houses, who makes an invaluable contribution to the building of new homes.[4]

Solid racism underpinned the economic arguments. It was only the black immigrants who were unwanted. It was only the black immigrants whom the government wished to exclude by the use of the 1962 Act. Labour's tepid opposition could not even rally to giving unconditional support to Fenner Brockway's Bill to Outlaw Racial Discrimination, blocked nine times by the Tory government. The final turning-point for Labour came, however, in 1964, when they lost a seat in Birmingham to a Tory campaigning on an overtly racist platform. 'Political expediency', as it was so delicately put, set Labour directly on course to win back the votes of racists, whom they appeased in 1965, in government, with further controls against immigration.

This left the Communist Party, for all its imperfections, as the only British political party in complete opposition to quotas and controls for Commonwealth immigration. Claudia Jones elaborated:

> ... all other parties have capitulated in one way or another to this racialist immigration measure. A recent statement of the Executive Committee of the British Communist Party declared its opposition to all forms of restrictions on coloured immigration; declared its readiness to contest every case of discrimination; urged repeal of

the Commonwealth Immigration Act; and called for equality of access for employment, rates of wages, promotion to skilled jobs, and opportunities for apprenticeship and vocational training. It gave full support to the Bill to Outlaw Racial Discrimination and pledged its readiness to support every single progressive measure to combat discrimination in Britain. It also projected the launching of an ideological campaign to combat racialism, which it noted, infects wide sections of the British working class.[5]

Integration – A Con Trick?

By the early sixties, it was clear to all that integration as a social goal had foundered completely. The right was open and provocative in its aggressive racism. The left, with precious few exceptions, was at best well-meaning and at worst hypocritical. Most people in between were simply uninformed or misinformed. As for those of us who had come to Britain to fulfil dreams, to contribute to struggle, to belong to a society which we thought we knew, we came to the conclusion that we had to operate both inside and outside the institutions of that society at the same time. This strategy was, in the first place, one which enabled us to survive in a hostile society. But in the second place, it was also the beginning of a strategy to change it. At our trade union branches, we would witness votes against employing more black workers and be told we didn't understand socialism if we mentioned racism. We retreated to our island organisations and informal caucuses for comfort and understanding. Gradually we saw that if we didn't fit the institutions of society, be they trade unions, parent-teacher groups, political parties or whatever, then the institutions didn't fit us either. They had all been designed without our presence, our experience and our interests in mind. We didn't necessarily disagree with them, we just wanted to participate on equal terms. Our own organisations began to change from places of retreat and defensiveness to places where a positive consolidation of our own identity could be forged. We came to see that the values and norms which excluded us from the mainstream of life were the values and norms of a deficient society.

A black teacher in the early sixties was talking to his class about the Commonwealth. He asked the children to put up their hand if they thought they were in the Commonwealth. The hands that shot up belonged to every one of the handful of black kids in the class. None of the white kids identified with the Commonwealth. That was a lesson for them all, the teacher included. Who were the real outsiders?

As Jeff Crawford, a community activist in north London, wrote in *Race Today* in 1972, summing up the black experience of the 'integration' period:

> Integration is a confidence trick. It is a conscious, deliberate, well-conceived plot to deceive, distract and divert us from our self-conceived objectives. The still trendy argument about trying to achieve integration is an empty one. Blacks are integrated already. The problem is one of discrimination ... Blacks have generally and rightly rejected all notions of assimilation and are instead demanding their unfettered human rights to participate on equal terms with the rest of the nation ... We were brainwashed into accepting that Britain was the Mother Country, the Mecca of civilisation where only good things happened and all the inhabitants were Christians, loving and benevolent ... Our demands will inevitably grow, leaving two options for white society, either give or refuse to give ...[6]

The concept of integration, in the abstract, seems perfectly laudable and plausible. What was wrong was the nature of the society in which it was hoped it could take place. In practice, it meant black people being integrated into a system of power, propped up by racism and wider inequalities, held in the hands of a tiny group of white men. Had we accepted that, we would have been accepting a future of total frustration and cutting ourselves off from any possibility of expressing our true selves. We would have been condemning ourselves to function as auxiliaries in society, not as equal members. We would have been even more exposed than we are anyway to being treated as pariahs and scapegoats when conflicts in society arose, or being patronised in the child-like way which brings comfort to white people's guilt. It is relatively painless for the white male power-base in this society to accept our prowess in cricket, as long as we are playing for the West Indies. But will they be able to cope with a predominantly black English cricket team? This is almost certain to be on the cards in the near future, and not only with cricket. Admiration and tolerance are one thing. Acceptance of black peoples' participation from a basis of equality is another. Between the two lies a power gap.

It was in the field of education that the black community first came to grips with exercising power over our own predicament, in order to lay the ground for challenging those who held themselves in power over us and our children's future. The next chapter records this stage of the struggle.

Notes

1. For further reading on Claudia Jones, *Caribbean News* and the *West Indian Gazette*, see Buzz Johnson, *I Think of my Mother: Notes on the Life and times of Claudia Jones*, Karia Press, 1985.
2. L. Constantine, *Colour Bar*, Paul and Co. Ltd., 1954.
3. Quoted in Johnson, op. cit.
4. Ibid.
5. Ibid.
6. J. Crawford 'Integration or Independence? A strategy for Black Groups', *Race Today*, Vol.4, No. 6, June 1972.

4 Different But Still Unequal

My daughter passed her eleven plus, but she insisted on going to the secondary modern school anyhow. She was frightened of racist jokes about coffee and cream she had heard from the grammar school kids. She threatened to run away if we sent her there. (A black mother)

The problem is now developing with almost every month that goes by, because we are beginning to move from the era of the first generation immigrant to that of the second generation immigrant. (Roy Jenkins, Home Secretary, May 1966)

The Commonwealth Immigration Act 1962 marked the end of the period characterised by the effort to 'integrate' and launched the West Indian community in Britain into a period of roughly a decade and a half which for us were positive and assertive years: the beginning of the fightback. By the mid-seventies, forty per cent of our community had been born here, though they were considered 'immigrants' just as we were.

In a House of Commons debate on race relations and immigration in 1973, Joan Lestor, Labour MP for Eton and Slough at the time, recounted a conversation she had heard in a nursery between a fifteen-year-old girl who was helping out and one of the white mothers. The girl's parents were West Indian. It was the kind of conversation which children like her were subjected to constantly. 'Where are you from, dear?' asked the mother. The girl replied, in a London accent, 'I am from Battersea.' 'No,' said the mother, 'where were you born?' The girl said, 'I was born in Wolverhampton.' The mother said, 'No, dear. I mean before that.'[1]

The experience which children from West Indian families,

whether they were born here or were immigrants, had in the education system presented us with a new dimension in our struggle against racism. The prospect of a good education was one of the main reasons for our emigration to Britain. But once our children entered the system in large numbers we found that not only were they not benefiting from the system we had held in such esteem, but they were actually considered to be so much of a threat to the stability and quality of the education service that policies were specifically designed to keep them as far on its margins as possible.

The extremely high expectations we had of the British education system need to be put into their historical context if other people are to understand more fully just how much of a slap in the face the racist education policies of the sixties were to us.

The end of the Second World War, although bringing peace and full employment in Europe, brought unemployment and its attendant miseries and problems to the vast majority of the people of the West Indies. Gone was the demand for certain raw materials that had been necessary for the war effort. Gone were the military bases on the islands. Together, these things had provided the people with something near to full employment and with comparatively high wages for the first time in their history. Against this background, the thousands of men and women who had participated in the struggle to stamp out fascism, Nazism and racism in Europe returning home.

They returned with a dream of a new world, free from poverty and inequality. Just as the troops returning home to Britain were promised 'a nation fit for heroes', so the West Indian troops expected a new order of things. But it was an unfulfilled dream. They went home to unemployment, not opportunities. Slavery and indentureship were long gone, but this did not mean people had achieved any real control over their own destiny. The post-emancipation period in the Caribbean had seen the plantation owners and imperial masters devising the most efficient ways to exploit the region's natural resources and extract as much wealth as possible from the colonial territories. Power they had, consent had to be won. The social structure, remnants of which remain today, was based on white power over the mass of angry, non-comforming freed slaves, backed up by the second tier in the power hierarchy consisting of the children born to black women by their white slave-masters. Indentured servants from India were introduced to soften the blow of the abolition of slavery and the refusal to work on the land by recalcitrant and angry ex-slaves. Religion and education played a crucial role, not only in socialising the people but also in the suppression and containment of further rebellion. The pay-off was that those who became 'good Christians', whether in the Protestant or Roman Catholic church, found it easier to be accepted into the educational institutions. Primary education was all that was on offer to the majority of people, with a tiny minority being accepted into the more prestigious colleges which were never meant for them.

Literacy, combined with participation in the dominant religion, resulted therefore in some black people gaining access to certain jobs, such as minor positions in the civil service, some office jobs, the teaching and nursing professions and the police force. In the minds of the majority of people, education was the key to upward mobility. The ideological control over education, however, was as tight as the economic stranglehold of the colonialist power. Seeking success and security through education meant accepting the dominant white imperialist culture and abandoning any affinity with African or Indian popular culture. What was British and white was best. What was of the people and black was ugly and bad.

Colonialism is potent. I believed there were certain occupations I could not enter. So I set my sights low. My choices were subject to the sanction of the white man. I was afraid to be right. Even if I was right, I needed the approval of the white man. On reflection, I can see that I grew up in a state of confusion. We only got schooling, not education. If you were colonising me, would you educate me?

I knew that because of my colour I couldn't get a job in a bank after leaving school in Guyana. In the civil service, I could expect to work only in certain departments. I was conscious that I couldn't get to the top, and of my mother's strong sense of grievance that her children couldn't achieve certain things. My white friends from school all got good jobs immediately.

Having identified education as the key to change, or at least as a means to an end, the dilemma faced by West Indians after the war was how to get it, as it was clearly not being handed to us on a plate at home. Some attempted to solve the problem politically, as indeed happened all over the colonial world, by struggling to wrest power away from the metropolitan country. Many others turned to migration in search of their key to the future. The door to North America was quickly shut by the McCarren Walter Act in 1952, which limited the number of British West Indians who could settle in the USA from 65,000 a year to only 800. People turned instead to Britain and exercised their rights, as their passports indicated, as 'British subject, Citizen of the United Kingdom and Colonies.'

The first three things most of us did as soon as we arrived were one, find the Labour Exchange, two, find a room and three, look for the nearest institute to register for evening classes. Wherever black people settled, adult education classes were full to the brim. But as the testimonies in the previous chapter have suggested, the strain of long hours in the factory by day eventually put paid to long hours of study by night for many of us. Another disappointment for some was the total lack of credit given for the education we had already received at home. It seemed that the great British education system only counted if you got through it on home ground. Back to square one again.

We had to leave the West Indies to get the educational grounding needed to enter the professions. It was very expensive at home, doing correspondence courses and importing books. But there were no exams to take, so we had to travel out. Then we discovered that even the Cambridge Certificate we had been groomed for at home was considered worthless in Britain. I was told it meant only that I could read and write, nothing more. I had been in building contracting at home, but here I was at the bottom of the pile.

The battle for our right to a good education and for equal treatment in the system also needs to be seen in the context of the increasing official panic over the level of immigration and the welter of conflicting legislation passed between the mid-sixties and mid-seventies, half designed to keep us out and make us feel vulnerable (and even more so our brothers and sisters from India, Pakistan and Bangladesh), and the other half (the series of Race Relations Acts in 1965, 1968 and 1976) to make us feel we had some measure of protection against discrimination. The Local Government Act 1966 also provided, through Section 11 grants, extra financial provision for local authorities providing services for Commonwealth immigrants.

Successive governments were terrified at the prospect of the 'British Way of Life' being swamped. In the 1964 General Election, the defeat of a Labour Minister in the Smethwick constituency by a Tory who campaigned under the slogan 'If you want a nigger for a neighbour, vote Labour', was the green light for the incoming Labour government to fall headlong into the same racist trap. Unable now to define anything as the problem except 'immigrants', they still clung pathetically to the notion of integration, but with a half-hearted hypocrisy typified by Roy Hattersley in 1965 when he said, 'Without limitation, integration is impossible.' Desperate at the same time to be seen as broad-minded, humanitarian and inclined towards equality of opportunity, the Labour government announced the existence of 'cultural diversity', which was to be respected. The real message behind 'cultural diversity' was: look, white Britain, they aren't going to go away, although we'll try not to let too many more come here. But as they're here to stay, we might as well accept that they like different things from us and let them get on with it. As long as they don't try to change us. Think of it as an interesting enrichment to our lives. We can have take-away curries and listen to the odd steel band. Wouldn't that be nice? If we tolerate them, they won't cause so much trouble.

Roy Jenkins tried to sell the new, improved version of the Race Relations Act in 1968 in this vein. Integration, he said, should be seen 'not as a flattering process of assimilation but equal opportunity, accompanied by cultural diversity, in an atmosphere of mutual tolerance'. Not that there was much sign of mutual tolerance visible at the time in the Labour Party's great ally, the trade union movement. The unions objected to employment discrimination being outlawed by the first Race Relations Act in 1965; the Act finally dealt solely with discrimination in 'public places'. The TUC also offered opposition to the second version of the Act in 1968, although employment along with housing were eventually included within its scope.

The lack of union support for the anti-discrimination legislation cannot be put down simply to the traditional – and up to a point, understandable – union resistance to workplace matters being resolved through the intervention of the law. The retirement speech which Sir William (later Lord) Carron gave in 1967 to the Amalgamated Engineering Union of which he was President revealed a depth of racist feeling and factual inacurracy which was not untypical in black peoples' experience:

> ... it would be interesting to obtain detailed statistics applying to the grand total that is consumed by educational grants, National Health and subsistence payments that become immediately obtainable by the ever-growing number of individuals who were not born in the country and who in no way contributed towards setting up a fund into which they so willingly dip their fingers. As they so succinctly put it, 'they know their rights'. It would be very acceptable to the rest of us if some small measure of appreciation and thanks were in visible evidence.

In the same year, the National Front was formed, with the twin aims of ending further immigration (by black people, that is) and of repatriating those already here. The NF's grass-roots activities, bolstered by Enoch Powell's infamous 'rivers of blood' speech in 1968, gave racism an unashamedly popular and open voice. Sections of the media seized on this and continued to play their part not only in reflecting, but in mobilising, 'public opinion'. Powell's speech closely echoed the sentiments expressed by the AEU's Sir William Carron, quoted above, accusing black immigrants of ousting 'Englishmen' from hospital beds, schools, houses and neighbourhoods and of taking liberties with their employers.

In the absence of any real labour movement opposition to this widespread racist campaign, the only national anti-racist organisation which attempted to combat it was the shortlived Campaign Against Racial Discrimination (CARD). But an organisation basically set up by a coalition of white liberals, Labour Party members and sections of the black middle class, working largely within a parliamentary framework, was no match for the hearts-and-minds, grass-roots type of politics in which the National Front was engaged. Some independent black organisations were involved, such as the Black Panthers and the Black Unity and Freedom Party, but these were also short-lived groups and hardly representative of a mass, class-based response from the black community.

In the opinion of some of the black people who were involved in CARD, it was doomed to failure because it was essentially an attempt by the (white) Labour Party machine to ape an American-style civil rights movement, which was inappropriate for the British political scene at the time, partly because of the lack of grass-roots political organisation within the black community demanding such a movement. Controlled by its white members, CARD effectively became a vehicle through which the Labour Party hoped to win more black votes. When black members tried to take control, the organisation was left to collapse and, in the words of one of its black activists, 'die a natural death'.

Black Power

While white politicians and others were concentrating on trying unsuccessfully to translate the influence of the American black civil rights movement to conditions in Britain, the black community responded to black American politics in its own way. While 'cultural diversity' was being wheeled out as sop to worried white liberals, we were doing something with our

cultural identity for ourselves. If the
inspiring, Black Power was even n
pursued as a serious political ideolog
simply as a trigger for individual pride

When the black American athlete
Olympics gave their Black Power salut
medals, thousands of black people
generation and our children's, felt we w
remember that occasion like they ...emember President
Kennedy's assassination: a symbolic moment in history. Our
collective political awareness as black people owed a great deal
to events in the USA.

In 1963 I saw a black civil rights march on television. That and the
Martin Luther King 'I have a dream' speech were very moving
experiences. It shook me into a kind of realisation that I was still
developing. It fermented my feelings and made me think in terms
of being black. I moved towards black groups and got involved in
the beginning of the supplementary school movement.

The civil rights movement and Black Power influenced me a lot,
but Michael X was not for me. I read all the books – Stokely,
Cleaver, Jackson. I respect Martin Luther King, although the civil
rights people were not as appealing to me as the militancy of Black
Power – much more exciting.*

Although one strand of the Black Power movement was to develop
black capitalism, the other strand which struck a chord with us in
the sixties in Britain was the way it created the political space for us
to redefine our own blackness and to develop a black perspective
to inject into the broader organisations and struggles in which we
were involved, such as over education or in the trade union
movement. Historically you could say it led to the demand for
black sections in unions and political parties. Black Power was
about pride and strength and solidarity, the rejuvenation of black
culture, a kind of renaissance and a recognition of the black
diaspora. It had a unifying effect between all age groups. The
older ones had to redefine their future and their past. We had to
decolonise ourselves.

* Michael X was Michael de Freitas, a Trinidadian living in London, who was
inspired by Malcolm X, the black American civil rights activist.

...unities which had been grim ghettoes in the fifties grew ...powerful political and cultural symbols for the black ...pulation. Reggae music, inspired by Bob Marley, became a black British phenomenon too, attracting and involving white as well as black youth. Black studies courses were demanded and started in both national and community educational institutions. The influence of Martin Luther King and other black church leaders contributed to the growth of black churches in communities all over Britain. Amongst the alienated youth, the emergence and growth of Rastafari was the most significant aspect of religious development. It was about more than just a religion, it was a whole black counter-culture.

Carnival in West London drew in more and more of the community, became a national cultural magnet and a local industry. This community was also fortunate to have the energy and dedication of Pansy Jeffries at its disposal. In 1959 she had become the first black worker ever to be employed by the Citizens Advice Bureaux. Sent to Ladbroke Grove as 'the black woman who looks after black people's problems' she works there to this day. During the sixties and seventies she was one of the driving forces behind numerous projects and organisations set up to cater for the social, housing and health needs of the West Indian community, particularly the women and children. A nurse and health visitor by training, her innovations included evening clinics for pregnant mothers who could not attend the regular daytime clinics because they were out at work. With West Indian music amongst the attractions, it was not long before white working class women took advantage of this provision as well.

Pansy was one of the founder members of the Notting Hill Housing Trust, possibly the first Housing Trust in which black people were involved. The Trust provided a building housing a Family Centre, used mainly by black senior citizens and unemployed girl school-leavers. 'Very much a women's effort', says Pansy, who taught them West Indian cookery and organised talks on black history for the youngsters. 'They knew nothing about the Caribbean or Africa, or their connection with either. We taught them, and it gave them confidence.' At one stage, a mobile resource bank of black learning materials was compiled – an ABC frieze with pictures of black children, a toy shop which had yams and cassava, for example. This was 'multi-cultural education' before the label had even been thought up!

Black Explosion

It was Haringey in North London, however, that became the symbol of resistance in the field of education from the end of the sixties. As the title of a *Race Today* pamphlet documenting the issues and events said, this was truly a 'Black Explosion'.[2] It was an explosion, however, whose impact seemed to bypass the white left and progressive movement altogether, despite the prominence of student politics at the same period which might have made the right connections. As it happened, it was the black struggle which set the pace for change and challenge to the education system as a whole over the next two decades.

Mass post-war immigration from the West Indies coincided with a period of intense experimentation in education in Britain. Secondary, further and higher education were being expanded and the development of a comprehensive system of secondary education was being debated and planned. There was instability in the teaching profession and a high turnover of teaching staff in schools, particularly in the run-down inner-city areas where we were forced to settle. Educational standards in these schools were *already* below the national norm and there was no policy (before the 1966 Local Government Act) for directing extra resources to such areas of need. All these factors had serious consequences for newly arrived children who had experienced a formal education in the West Indies, where school teachers were amongst the most well known, respected and stable figures in the community, familiar to and trusted by parents.

To begin with, we – the parents – were baffled. Our children were not succeeding as we expected, but our lack of knowledge about the education system and our defensive unwillingness to believe that racism was to blame, tempted us to think that something might indeed be wrong with us or our children. I remember reacting with amusement when my own children came home from school deeply upset because the teachers had told them to go home to the jungle. I just couldn't believe that a teacher would say that sort of thing except as an innocent joke. The children would also say how their teachers found it difficult to engage in any conversation with them. I and my contemporaries, however, were still labouring under the illusion that these schools and these teachers were good for our children. When the children told the truth about their sufferings from racism, we simply could not see it. It even took time for us to develop respect for the few black teachers we came across. At first, it was the white teachers we sought out to discuss our 'problem' children with. We assumed they knew best. Only when it became clear that they were, on the whole, on a completely different wavelength from us did we turn to the black teachers and begin to understand that we were in the same sinking boat and that we needed to form an alliance to save ourselves and our children.

When it took off, that alliance showed that it was capable of being powerful and effective, despite the odds against us.

It was the Asian community in Southall which was the first to be subjected to the racist directives from the politicians responsible for education in this country. White parents in Southall, West London, went onto the attack by complaining about large numbers of Asian children in 'their' schools. This led to the official policy of 'dispersal', which decreed that where a school consisted of more than 30 per cent 'immigrant' children, allegedly making the school a bad school, then the surplus number of children were to be bussed further afield to other schools. This exercise was soon to be repeated at the expense of children from West Indian families in Haringey and elsewhere. For those with any trace of sympathy left for the idea of integration, this was the last straw.

The 1963 offensive against Asian children in Southall was consolidated in 1965 by a DES circular confirming the policy of dispersal to reassure worried white parents. It said:

As the proportion of immigrant children in a school or class increases, the problems will become more difficult to solve, and the chances of assimilation more remote ... up to a fifth of immigrant children in any one group fit with reasonable ease, but if the proportion goes over about one-third in the school as a whole or in any one class, serious strains arise.[3]

Put bluntly, what this statement meant was that black children *en masse* are ineducable and therefore create problems for teachers and other children. It simply did not occur to the powers that be that the real problem lay in the inadequacy of the system to meet the needs of black children, children who could bring to the institution positive cultural experiences which would enhance the life of the school and the education of the other children. The word 'assimilation' in this context implied that black people could only be assimilated into the education system if they were in minorities and monolingual. Very little thought was given at the time to the now more commonplace idea that the school should function as a part of the community and be understood as such by both parents and children. On the contrary, the policy of dispersal only increased their alienation from the social institution where they should have been experiencing a constructive relationship and partnership with all concerned. It was not difficult to see through the official claptrap about black children lowering educational standards. After all, no one had ever proposed bussing white working class children who were failing academically in the inner city to other schools with a better record of achievement.

The DES circular prepared the ground for several local education authorities to introduce a policy of dispersal, which took the form of bussing black children and which led to the first direct confrontation between an LEA and West Indian parents. Our consciousness as black parents was stimulated and galvanised into action, on the one hand by the practical impact on our children of such increasingly blatant and inescapably racist policies; and, on the other by the pioneering campaigning work of black mothers and black professionals in the fields of teaching and community work, who formulated and publicised a black perspective on what was happening. The last piece of the jigsaw finally fell into place for me in 1969 when I read 'Violence in the Toilets', an article by black teacher Marina Maxwell.[4] Her article was an angry and emotional response to a study by the National Council for Commonwealth Immigrants called *The Education of West Indian Immigrant Children*, which had concluded:

> ... there is little doubt that many [West Indian] children suffer from an acute sense of insecurity which, abetted by the general uncertainty, deprivation and malnutrition of their environment at home, produces a type of personality lacking in concentration and a sense of application.[5]

That was clear and calculated disrespect for the black family. The racism there finally cut to the quick in those of us who had been holding on to some degree of faith in the education system. Marina Maxwell's article (with its title which derived from one of her teacher colleagues' statements that black pupils preferred to hang around in the toilets during the lunch break rather than engage in any other activities, which were not therefore worth organising for them) hit back with the force of one who, as a teacher herself, felt hurt, confused, isolated and frustrated by racism in education. She said:

> History repeats itself in a nauseating and nauseated circle – talk about the planters and missionaries commenting in the West Indies and Africa on the pre-ordained inferiority of the Blacks. If the writers of this pamphlet knew anything of the West Indies and the triumphant survival of the West Indian migrant societies all over the world, despite unholy odds, they could never make such ridiculous statements. They are laying the framework for teachers to be indifferent and intolerant and for the society to reinforce its already racialistic tendencies.
>
> Britain, especially London, like it or not, is reaping the results of the glorious Empire, and internationalism has happened. Instead of the blinkered resentment that can only lead to race riots, why not tackle the problem?

Maxwell pointed to the inadequacy of teacher training in a multi-racial society, the racism built in to teachers' attitudes and the racism of the curriculum: all the factors which (as we shall see in the last chapter) it was to take the establishment almost another twenty years (and how many more 'failed' black children?) to acknowledge as an accurate description of the failures of the system itself. (And even then, the Swann Report, which finally came clean on racism in education, was immediately disowned by the Secretary of State for Education.)

Marina Maxwell's bitterness, however, led her to pessimistic conclusions and it was this that signalled to me that we had reached a stage of urgency in relations between the black community and the education system. Her message to the black community was: 'If you know anyone back home who is thinking of coming over, tell them firmly, for your children's sake, don't migrate to England!' This view was shared by others in the community, particularly parents and community workers. Maxwell herself eventually returned home to Trinidad. By this time, however, most of us had faced up to the fact that we were here for good. The three, four and five years we had originally intended to stay were long gone. Our children and their future were here. Our struggles and commitments were here. And of course, for some of us, our mortgages were here and hardly likely to be charitably withdrawn should we pack up and go home.

From the hurt and anger quickly sprang strength and organisation. The alliance between black parents, black teachers, social and community workers – and some measure of white liberal and anti-racist support – was tested and vindicated in Haringey, North London, from 1969. Superficially, the issue was the proposal to bus black children around the borough to avoid the development of 'ghetto' schools which, it was imagined, would have 'far reaching social and educational repercussions'. The campaign, spearheaded by the North London West Indian Association (NLWIA), was successful in getting the plan scrapped. But the challenge of the black activists went deeper and turned the issues of the campaign into the focus of national concern instead of simply a local problem.

The NLWIA was already a well established organisation, part of a network of local groups all over the country which were affiliated to the umbrella organisation, the West Indian Standing Conference, which itself had been formed after the 1958 race riots. The NLWIA was a black, working class organisation with a great deal of campaigning experience to its credit, spanning employment, educational and community issues. Its most recent success had been in 1968 when it took on London Transport and the Transport and General Workers' Union over their refusal to back the promotion of Lionel Franklin, a black worker, to be an inspector. There were no black inspectors at all at the time. The NLWIA used its contacts in bus garages across London to mobilise enough support to threaten a 24-hour strike by black crews. They won.

Interest in educational issues was not new to the NLWIA either. They had been setting up black parents' groups in North London since the mid-sixties, in response to the growing need for information, solidarity and self-help amongst black parents who could not understand their children's lack of progress at school. In 1969, alongside the bussing question, the NLWIA identified the practice of banding children according to academic ability as part of the same racist policies which were setting up our children for failure. Banding may appear to be an administratively convenient, even educationally sensible, idea to many teachers faced with a mixed ability school population. But in the context of educational research and practice which assumes an inherent deficiency in the ability of black children, banding operates as an instrument of institutionalised racism.

When I became a teacher in the early seventies, the image I formed of the academic structure of my first (secondary) school, in which the majority of pupils were black, was of a snow-capped mountain. At the top, the white headteacher and most of the staff (I was the only West Indian teacher). Immediately below, the white children. Then the black children, concentrated at the base of the mountain, a long way from the snow.

Barbare Beese and Leila Hassan published an account of the campaign against banding in *Race Today*. This is how they summarised the provocation to the black community and its organised response.

The real motivation behind the banding proposals was revealed in a confidential report by the Vice-Chairman of the Education Committee, Alderman A.J.F. Doulton, who was also Headmaster of the public Highgate School. He said, 'On a rough calculation about half of the immigrants will be West Indian at seven of the eleven schools, the significance of this being the general recognition that their IQs work out below their English contemporaries. Thus academic standards will be lower in schools where they form a large group.'

The report also called attention to the increasing tendency of immigrant pupils to stay on beyond the school-leaving age and the consequent growth of non-academic sixth forms. 'It is a process that will continue and it could particularly affect Haringey where the immigrant parents will see education as the way to open doors for their children.' He was expressing the apprehensions of those like himself who feared that under the comprehensive system of education, large numbers of blacks who were living in the area would swamp their middle-class white schools.

Three days after the official report was released, NLWIA organised the first protest demonstration ever staged by Haringey's West Indian community outside the Borough's Civic Centre. Pamphlets were run off and distributed, open meetings for parents were held, parents' committees formed, a televised national press conference was called and a protest petition containing the signatures of 928 local West Indian parents was handed in to the Council. An alliance was also made with the white middle-class residents in the Borough who opposed the banding scheme for their own reasons. Through them, however, the NLWIA had access to confidential reports and media contacts. The Conservative controlled Haringey Borough Council implemented banding for a short time, but with a change to a new Labour-controlled council, in May 1971, and in the face of the mass mobilisation of the black community on this issue, the Labour Party decided the scheme would be dropped.

As a result of the campaign against banding, the community's consciousness on the issue of education was heightened considerably. Now, all over England, black parents started to agitate against what was taking place in schools. They were well prepared for the next assault which was to come over channelling of black children in Educationally Sub-Normal Schools (ESN).[6]

In fact, the NLWIA had been aware of the ESN problem since the mid-sixties. In the Inner London Education Authority by 1967, immigrant children formed 28.4 per cent of the pupils in ESN schools, compared to 15 per cent in ordinary schools. And out of all immigrant children (West Indian, Indian, Pakistani, Cypriot and others) in ESN schools, no fewer than 75 per cent were West Indians, although they made up only 54 per cent of the immigrant population of ordinary schools.

This grotesque distortion had been achieved by effectively conning West Indian parents who were offered 'special education' for their children. The word 'special' meant one thing to professionals familiar with educational jargon and something completely different to the uninformed West Indian parents who thought they were being offered a good service, something special. Haringey's Education Committee admitted to the NLWIA in 1969 that immigrant children had indeed been wrongly assessed and classified as educationally sub-normal, but the Authority was not prepared to remedy the situation. The NLWIA responded by complaining to the Race Relations Board (RRB), which had been set up by the 1965 Race Relations Act. The Council retaliated by making its own complaint to the RRB, accusing the NLWIA of racism by excluding white parents from its meetings. Under Jeff Crawford's leadership, the NLWIA refused to co-operate with the investigation into this complaint and nothing more was heard of it.

It took the RRB over a year to reach the disgraceful conclusion that the local authority had not breached the law in wrongly assessing West Indian children as ESN. But it is possible that this decision unwittingly contributed to the momentum and strengthening of the black movement in education on a national scale. Weeks after the Board's announcement, a pamphlet was published, based on a paper given at a conference the year before, 1970, organised by the Caribbean Education and Community Workers Association. The author was Bernard Coard (later deputy Prime Minister in revolutionary Grenada); the pamphlet, now familiar as a classic text to all those involved in multi-cultural and anti-racist education, was called *How the West Indian Child is Made Educationally Sub-normal in the British School System.*[1] Today, over fifteen years later, this pamphlet is still essential reading and should without doubt or hesitation be on the compulsory reading list for all teachers and teachers-to-be in all British schools, whether or not they have black children on their rolls.

Bernard Coard, a Grenadian-born teacher with professional experience in ESN schools and youth clubs in London, analysed with great clarity the impact of what we later came to label the 'institutional racism' in the education system, which prescribed the failure of black children and perpetuated the position of the black community as the most socially and economically disadvantaged section of society. He described the cultural bias of IQ assessment for ESN schools, based on a white, middle-class norm against which our children were bound to be found lacking. He described how relegation to ESN schools was a permanent sentence to the outer margins of possible achievement in both education and employment. He described, in perhaps the most striking and poignant section of the pamphlet, both his personal experience as a teacher and the research studies which had revealed the devastatingly low self-esteem of black children, fuelled by the absence of any positive black images within the educational setting and by the racist attitudes of white teachers, ranging from patronising remarks to outright refusal to teach 'those niggers'.

The pamphlet concludes with a detailed strategy for reversing the trend of dumping West Indian children in ESN schools. It also exhorts black parents to get more involved with their children's schools and education generally. Most significantly, Coard called on the black community to act collectively by establishing supplementary schools:

We need to open Black nursery schools and supplementary schools throughout the areas we live in, in Britain. Our nursery schools should have Black dolls and toys and pictures, and storybooks about great Black men and women, and their achievements and inventions. Our children need to have a sense of identity, pride and belonging, as well as mental stimulation, so that they do not end up hating themselves and their race, and being dumped in ESN schools. Pride and self-confidence are the best armour against the prejudice and humiliating experience which they will certainly face in school and in society.

We should start up supplementary schools in whatever part of London, or Britain, we live, in order to give our children additional help in the subjects they need. These classes can be held on evenings and Saturday mornings. We should recruit all our Black students and teachers for the task of instructing our children. Through these schools we hope to make up for the inadequacies of the British school system, and for its refusal to teach our children our history and culture. We must never sit idly by while they make ignoramuses of our children, but must see to it that by hook or crook our children get the best education they are capable of! Some supplementary schools have already been started in parts of London. Don't be the last to get your child in one!

As Barbara Beese and Leila Hassan pointed out:

The response was fantastic. 10,000 copies were sold. Coard spoke up and down the country. There was enormous press, TV and radio coverage, including the international press. Supplementary schools were formed in all the major cities with large black populations. It was clear that this was an issue which black communities throughout England were aware of and were mobilising to do something about. No one had to go and organise them around the issue in order to convince them that they should do something.

Supplementary Schools

The mass growth of supplementary schools, like many other social innovations, represented an idea whose time had come. The influences which surrounded their development were many and varied, but it was the Coard pamphlet that crystalised the motivation of black parents and teachers on a national scale. There were certainly a few supplementary schools in existence even before the battle lines were drawn in Haringey and it is difficult to state which were the first. Certainly there was one established in Shepherds Bush, West London, as early as 1967, which has been acknowledged by Steven Delsol in a brief pamphlet on the subject.[8] The Shepherds Bush Supplementary School was opened on Tuesday and Thursday evenings by Clinton Sealy, out of concern for the many black children he saw in the streets after school because their parents were still out at work. Maureen Stone in her book *The Education of the Black Child in Britain* (1981) drew an analogy between the black supplementary school movement and the Socialist Sunday school movement in the late nineteenth and early twentieth centuries.[9] The Socialist Sunday Schools:

> offered to working class children the means to foster a self-image based, not on therapy or charity, but on hard work, disciplined study and the will to succeed. Just as the Socialist Sunday Schools were mainly organised and run by working class people for working class children, so also in the West Indian Saturday schools we find ordinary working class people who, as part-time teachers, are 'demystifying' the teaching and learning process as part of the response to a social structure and its institutions which discriminate against them and their children.

The Socialist Sunday School movement eventually disintegrated as a result of sectarian disagreements amongst the various political strands of the leadership. One of the many reasons for its collapse was the failure to involve adequately the parents of the children whom the movement aimed to instil with working class consciousness and a commitment to socialism. In a way, the supplementary school movement is the ideological successor to the Socialist Sunday Schools, aiming as it does both to counteract the discrimination of the mainstream education system and to develop black consciousness in the children. The political ideology of supplementary

schools is far more diverse than the earlier white socialist
movement, with schools being run by community groups
ranging from Rastafarians to Seventh Day Adventists and many
others with no political or religious affiliation at all. It is my
own hope that specifically socialist supplementary schools
might also one day develop. And if the failure to capture the
parents along with their children was one of the shortcomings
of the Socialist Sunday Schools, the unity, trust and
co-operation between the generations within our own black
supplementary school movement could be, by contrast, its
lasting strength. Black consciousness welded to socialist
commitment could just be the historic catalyst which could
bring about the 'opportunity of a healthy and happy life for
all' dreamed of at the turn of the century by our predecessors
in supplementary education.

Supplementary schools are a partnership between teachers,
parents and children. Different schools have different
emphases, some concentrating on the 'three Rs' in order to
compensate for the conscious or unconscious neglect of their
children's basic academic development in mainstream schools
and in the belief that proficiency in the dominant culture will
best enable our children to compete and succeed on equal
terms in a hostile society. The presence of black adults,
teachers and others, is also seen as fundamentally important,
providing the children with role models who help create the
motivation to succeed. Other schools concentrate on a 'black
studies' approach, designed to give the children the kind of
historical and cultural knowledge of their own people which
they could never hope to gain from mainstream schooling.
What a difference it makes to a black child to learn of African
and West Indian history – and from a black perspective. The
names of many supplementary schools reflect this emphasis:
Albertina Sylvester, George Padmore, Kwame Nkrumah and
George Washington Carver gave their names to four of the first
schools in London. Many schools, of course, provide a mixture
of 'straight' academic work combined with black history and
culture, sometimes from a specifically religious perspective.

The confidence and security which the supplementary school

engenders in the children makes it much more likely that they will achieve more in the mainstream school. The black teachers in supplementary schools tend to see a completely different side of a child's character from the white teacher in 'normal' school:

I taught in a supplementary school in Hackney which was held every Wednesday evening. There was one boy with a 'naughty' reputation, whose behaviour was completely different in the supplementary school. At ordinary school he would give up very quickly, get into mischief and generally be anti-social. But at supplementary school, he became part of everything. He took pride in whatever work he was given to do and I certainly observed a feeling of self-respect in him. There were another two boys who I could see weren't being stretched by school work. They were both from one-parent families, whose fathers had died suddenly. There were four or five children in each family. Their mothers were very hardworking but were often in hospital. The supplementary school provided an environment in which these boys could use their talents. There was another youngster with whom I used to have long conversations in the evenings, about race and the condition of black people all over the world. He felt alienated from ordinary school and hated both it and the teachers for a period. He fell into a group of similar kids and got involved in petty thieving. I knew that behaviour was really alien to him, but his white teachers, while not nasty to him, just gave up hope. They couldn't feel the concern for him or his family the way I could. They thought he should leave school in his own and the other kids interests. This boy later got to university.

Whatever the grouping behind a supplementary school, religious or community, the main objectives are to motivate the children to succeed in mainstream school and to equip the children with sufficient knowledge of their history to meet the future with confidence. In theory, of course, this is exactly what all children should receive ordinarily at school. But the vicious circle of racism giving rise to low expectations of black children, leading to their academic under-achievement, is a tough nut to crack, especially given the inadequacy of teacher training for the needs of children in a multi-racial inner-city area. At the period when supplementary schools began to spring up, there was very little recognition amongst white teachers or in the system as a whole of the problem *as an institutional one*. The failure was presumed to be that of the black children and their families. By contrast, the success of children who have had their schooling supplemented by their own community's efforts has been shown through an improved rate of O level passes. This success has not yet been subject to any statistical scrutiny, but is certainly to the credit of supplementary schools in the eyes of the experienced black teachers.

Children are by no means the only people to gain from the supplementary school movement. Teachers and parents also reap positive benefits. The schools provide a special space and function for young black teachers. They acquire useful professional skills that their usually low status in the mainstream school hierarchy prevents them from developing, particularly from a managerial point of view. They can take the kind of decisions about their own work and about the children in their care from which they would normally be excluded in their main job. Further, the emphasis on partnership with parents in the supplementary school set-up helps in confidence building for the young teachers. Most important of all is the understanding that their own life chances are inextricably tied up with the life of their community.

For parents, involvement with a supplementary school provides a stark contrast with their experience of mainstream schools, where the main structural links between parents and teachers are Parent Teacher Associations. Few PTAs in inner-city areas, however, are successful in enabling a genuine partnership between their two constituencies to flourish. In most cases, they are dominated by parents who either share the values of the teachers, or who have the time to participate and are articulate enough to disentangle and interpret the code and jargon in which teachers communicate with each other.

It is the experience of many black parents that the fundamental questions about their children's education are never really answered. Effectively, this means they feel discouraged from participating in a meaningful way in their children's educational life. No doubt many white working class parents feel similarly excluded or undermined. But black parents found in supplementary schools a way round the wall of silence, for these schools were deliberately constructed on the basis of quite different assumptions about parental participation. It is actively encouraged in educational, planning and management terms.

Of immense value in itself, this level of involvement has also had the spin-off of giving black parents the knowledge and confidence to intervene in and challenge the mainstream system. The renewed sense of comradeship which supplementary schools have enhanced amongst groups of black parents has been essential in the struggle to defend the whole black community's right to a good education. But the significance of supplementary schools relates to more than the black community alone. As Maureen Stone has put it, 'They represent perhaps the only real example of working class community involvement in schooling at the present time.'

Black Teachers

It was during the late sixties that I decided to become a teacher in secondary education. Job satisfaction being underemployed in a factory was nil. My community activity prevented me from pursuing evening classes properly. So after getting three A levels, I turned to teacher training. I felt that given the problems of the black community I could marry teaching with work in the community. To me, there was in any case no difference or demarcation between the two. I saw it as killing two birds with one stone. It took some time to come to terms with, on the one hand, the difference in cultural values between myself and the black children I taught and, on the other, to work out the best ways of exploiting, to our mutual advantage, the similarities in our experience and perceptions of the world. They had no automatic affinity with me just because I was black too. And I was wary of them. They saw me as part of the system: on the staff, therefore the enemy. So their first response was one of resistance.

Once I realised that this sense of resistance was the cultural and historical bond between us, something which I shared rather than needed to feel threatened by, I began to identify with them. In me, the culture of resistance had been nurtured through growing up on a colonial island. In them it grew from survival on the streets in a working class, inner-city area of an industrialised society. But once the children saw that I was able to identify with them and could see me as part of them, a solid trust developed. They were even protective towards me, coming to my defence if they believed I had been the victim of personal or institutional racism. They would often ask me why I wasn't Head of Department and brush aside any explanation I offered, saying it could only be racism.

As a teacher in a large boys' comprehensive school in East London, I knew I would have to deal with the racist behaviour of white working class kids. But one day it was I who learned a lesson about racism. Going into the fourth year classroom, I immediately noticed a caricatured drawing on the blackboard of the head of a Jewish man, with 'Jewish bastard' written underneath. I instantly assumed one of the white boys was responsible and bellowed at the class for him to own up. The boys generally felt sufficient respect towards me for me to feel confident that the culprit would soon stand up. Nothing happened. So I applied the usual second tactic and said I would leave the room for a few minutes to give them a chance to discuss the situation, assuming this would create enough pressure for the guilty boy to own up.

During my few minutes' grace outside in the corridor, I planned to use the situation to discuss racism and fascism in the classroom, using the Holocaust as the theme. I went back in and, as I expected, the boy responsible for the racist caricature stood up. It was a black lad. I certainly had to think on my feet at that moment and I was really quite fazed by my confusion. What I had not taken into account was that the social and political history and culture of this part of London was bound to be reflected in the culture of the school; and contrary to many peoples' belief, there remains a legacy of anti-Semitism. The main lesson I learned was that the black children's minds were just as open as the white children's minds to negative ideas, even though there was no historical reason for them to feel anti-semitic. It was this incident more than any other which strengthened my resolve to work alongside those white colleagues who were calling for an anti-racist policy for the school.

As a teacher, I quickly learned that many of my white colleagues, although reasonable people, could rely on nothing in their background or their professional training to help them deal with teaching mixed classes of black and white children. It was easy to get some of them to sit down and talk about developing an anti-racist policy statement for the school and changing the curriculum. What was difficult to win was their recognition of a hidden curriculum, and that that hidden curriculum mattered. Swimming against the tide of scores of years of practice and habit made us, the few black teachers, feel vulnerable, while white colleagues felt threatened. Their resistance, both to change in general and to confronting their own racism, was natural. We had to look outside the immediate environment of the school to mobilise support.

The starting point was with ourselves, as black teachers. An organisation which later became the Caribbean Teachers' Association (CTA) was formed in 1972, for mutual solidarity and support. We also wanted to increase the desperately small number of black teachers in the education service. The CTA had traced only 383 West Indian teachers in the whole country and estimated a total of no more than 800 overall. Our purpose was, however, not confined to the promotion of our own interests as professionals who were the victims of discrimination in our employment, clustered in the lower scales of payment and status. Our aims were to provide role models for black children, to help black parents develop their involvement with their children's schools, and to provide a positive image for white people too, combating their stereotyped images of black people.

Members of the CTA also worked in and alongside organisations set up by groups of white, anti-racist teachers, including Teachers Against Racism, the National Association for Multi-Racial Education (NAME, later to become the National Anti-Racist Movement in Education) and the All London Teachers against Racism and Fascism.

The other organisations of which we were, of course, all members, were our trade unions, principally the NUT. To many white teachers, the NUT was simply the vehicle for winning better pay and conditions, no more and no less. It took a good deal of courage for a black teacher to make a conscious effort to participate in an organisation which always seemed to relegate the race dimension of black teachers' conditions of work to 'any other business'. Like some of the industrial and craft unions which many of us had been involved with when we first came to Britain, the NUT got to the stage of passing national resolutions about racism. But at grass-roots level, the practice remained relatively untouched by the theory. Discussion with white colleagues was often very difficult. They had arrived at their anti-racist position via political theory, not through any direct experience of racism. Their policies and practices were therefore uninformed by the reality of life for the black teacher and seemed, to us, confused.

For example, my union branch put up a motion to national conference which incorporated a statement of commitment to anti-racism in education, *together with* a call to repeal all immigration laws. By incorporating the section on immigration, the motion was effectively condemned to fall. My own arguments to separate out the two elements of the motion, in the interests of getting through the valuable and constructive commitment on anti-racist education practices, which would have achieved a real effect on the daily lives of black teachers and pupils, were attacked as reactionary.

One of the first things the CTA did when it formed in 1972 was to invite ourselves to meet the Executive Committee of the NUT to discuss race. Three-quarters of the Executive turned out. But this encouraging sign betrayed their ignorance of and resistance to almost everything we had to put to them. We were lobbying for a union policy on race discrimination against black teachers. No need, we were told: all teachers are equal.

We wanted a union policy on multi-ethnic and anti-racist education. No need, we were told: teachers don't see black children and white children, just children. We came away extremely frustrated, with some of our members inclined to abandon the NUT altogether and work solely through the CTA.

The majority, however, resolved to initiate an ideological struggle to confront and change racist attitudes among white teachers. This was quite a task when even the left-liberal teachers whom we considered to be our allies seemed fundamentally to share the views expressed by our Union's Executive Committee. Within a few years, the combination of black pressure, internal white anti-racist pressure and the existence and activities of NAME, shifted the NUT significantly to a relatively progressive stance on race. Frustrating as those few years were, we did learn that by playing our part in the union, we could make it change to reflect the wishes of all its members, including the black teachers.

One of the key differences in understanding between the black teachers and our white colleagues arose from the extent to which we shared a common experience outside school with the black children we taught, whereas the white teachers shared little in the way of values, lifestyle, perceptions and daily experiences on the street with the children they taught, black or white.

How could the average white teacher envisage the black children he or she assumed were disruptive, indisciplined and virtually ineducable as, for example, conscientious young members of their Pentecostal Church? If the left isn't recruiting black youth, the black churches certainly are. I was invited, in 1980, to address the Afro-West Indian Organisation of Churches, in my capacity as chair of the Caribbean Teachers' Association. I thought it would be a small meeting in a small room. It turned out to be a massive hall, with the capacity for thousands. And it was standing-room only. I sat on the platform in awe. The gathering represented the outlawed black church from the West Indies as I had known it as a child. Sober-suited men and women with hats bearing cherries and dates mingled with others looking like Moses in robes of purples and mauves. The speeches were out of this world and there were four choirs. After I had made my speech, a young woman of about 18 or 19 came up to me and said 'Hello sir'. I had taught her in the sixth form. It struck me then that the kids in those choirs were the same kids our schools couldn't handle. They had to turn up for practice three times a week for a start. The whole experience boosted my confidence in my own people and taught me not to dismiss the church lightly.

Relations with the police was the prime example of the difference in experience between black people and white people. Out on the streets, no one, police officers least of all, knew us as teachers. We were just blacks, subject to the same racial harassment and abuse as the pupils over whom we exercised some degree of power and control in the classroom.

As a teacher of social studies, I had to deal with the topic of 'law and order'. In 1972, the school's policy was to invite police officers in to speak to the third-year pupils about their jobs. At first, I was naive enough to believe that under the teacher's guidance and controlled by the curriculum, these sessions had a useful educational role. One afternoon's lesson put paid to that. Four policemen came into the school. During the discussion, one black boy began to describe his recent experience of being arrested. He had been standing at a bus stop and witnessed some other lads breaking a shop window and running away. Together with an elderly, white woman at the bus stop, he went over to look at the damage. Within minutes the police arrived and, without asking any questions, held the boy, taking no notice of his protestations of innocence, despite the support of the old lady. She was just told to shut up. The boy was bundled into the police car and taken to the station. Fortunately, someone who knew him had seen everything, went with the old lady to inform his parents and the entire group went to the police station. Eventually, they were able to convince the officers of the boy's innocence.

In my classroom that afternoon, the boy challenged the police. Did they think it was right, he asked, that he should

have been picked up so unjustly? To a man, they disputed the
story. They quizzed him as if he were under arrest again, but he
stuck to his guns. When they realised they were not going to
catch him out, they changed tack and said that whilst the police
were right in most cases, there had obviously been some
mistake here. All this was said without one iota of sympathy for
the boy or his family. Their behaviour took no account
whatsoever of their school surroundings or the purpose of
their visit: they just carried on like a bunch of officers in their
interrogation room. I pointed this out and said I thought they
were achieving exactly the opposite of what was intended by
the session. No way were they breaking down barriers or
building the kids' confidence in the police. The startled looks
on their red, embarrassed faces told me they realised they had
blundered. For my part, I knew I would never forget the sight
of this third-year black kid holding forth against four
policemen at his articulate best. Neither would I forget the
looks of incredulity on the faces of the rest of the class. I knew I
had to pick up the pieces. I would certainly need to find a
different approach to 'law and order'.

The Police

If my social studies class revealed an individual crisis between
one black child and four policemen, relations between the
police and the black community as a whole were becoming a
national scandal. Persecution is not too strong a word to
describe the daily treatment at the hands of the police
experienced by young black men in particular. In the first
place, they were more exposed to contact with the police on the
streets, since the levels of young black male unemployment
were double that for white youth. The 1971 census showed a
16.2 per cent unemployment rate for boys born in the West
Indies, compared to an 8 per cent national average. The figure
for young black men born here of West Indian parents was not
significantly lower. Young women fared slightly better than
young men in the job market and in any case were less likely to
register as unemployed, as with all young women at that time.

The second factor was the racism amongst the overwhelmingly white police force. Even Roy Jenkins, as Home Secretary addressing the House of Commons in 1973 in a debate on race relations, levelled a pointed if understated challenge to the police over their attitudes. He noted that, since 1966 when the first 'coloured' police officer was recruited to the Metropolitan Police, only a further seventy-odd had been recruited – less than one-tenth of 1 per cent of the force. 'That bears no relation to the fact that approximately 3 per cent of the population is coloured,' he said. He went on to hope there had been some improvement in police attitudes to welcoming black colleagues within their ranks since an annual police conference he had attended in 1966 when he had spoken about the desirability of black recruitment. His words, he said, had been 'greeted with a noise which I did not take to be the sound of enthusiasm.'[10]

The third factor behind the crisis between the police and the black community was the existence of the 'sus law' which gave ample room for the police to vent their racist prejudices. Despite actual crime rates for the black community being below the average for the white population, black people, particularly the young, were virtually assumed to be criminal or potentially criminal by the police on the streets. The 'sus' charge, as it was known, derived from part of the 1824 Vagrancy Act and was used effectively to clear the streets of young people whom the police suspected were loitering with intent to commit an arrestable offence. Those accused had no right to be tried by jury. Black people accounted for a higher proportion of those arrested on 'sus' than their numbers in the population as a whole. As John la Rose, owner of the New Beacon bookshop in North London, said in 1970, 'No black people are free from police brutality. If you haven't been arrested, it merely means you haven't been arrested yet.' The early seventies also saw high profile racist campaigns against mugging organised by the National Front and a great deal of media coverage of Enoch Powell's latest onslaught against the black community in his definition of mugging as a black crime. 'Mugging' was in fact a term which the media – especially the

London *Evening Standard* – did much to create from 1971 onwards. 'Mugging' has no legal meaning.

If 'sus' didn't get you, you could bet on at least being stopped and searched by the Special Patrol Group. Probably quite often. That stop and search activity constituted unwarranted harassment is suggested easily by the figures for subsequent arrests. In 1972, for example, out of 41,980 people stopped and searched, only 3,142 were arrested. In 1975, out of 18,907 stop and searches in Greater London, 14,000 were in Lambeth and Lewisham alone, over a two-month period. This assault on two of London's biggest black communities resulted in just 403 arrests.

The black community in North Kensington also suffered from disproportionate use of 'sus' and stop and search police powers. There had not been much love lost between the police and the black community since the unsolved murder of Kelso Cochrane in 1959 and the subsequent race riots. The focal point symbolising the tension from the late sixties (and to this day) was the Mangrove restaurant in All Saints Road, Notting Hill Gate.

Opened in 1969 by Frank Crichlow, a Trinidadian who had come to Britain in 1953 at the age of 20, the Mangrove was more than just a restaurant. In Frank's words, it was – and still is – 'a community organisation'. The bulletins from the nearby Black Peoples' Information Centre during the spectacular ten-week trial of the Mangrove Nine in 1971 went further in their description of the Mangrove, calling it 'a black community centre and a centre of resistance to police repression'. Frank Crichlow had never intended an overtly political role for the Mangrove, seeing it more as a social centre, mainly for West Indians, but also for local white people. 'A social centre where people can thrash out their problems and discuss them,' was how one of Frank's character witnesses in the Mangrove Nine trial put it. But black-initiated self-help in a society beset with racist attitudes was bound to offer more to its community than the familiarity and comfort of West Indian music and food.

One journalist rightly described the Mangrove as 'an oasis in

a hostile and uncomprehending environment'. Frank was
well-established in the local community. He had opened the
Rio coffee bar in 1960 and the Mangrove was its successor.
Both places were popular meeting places as well as eating
places and attracted for many years a custom which included
the trendy and chic – black and white – as well as the local,
young, black working class. Unlike many other black club and
restaurant owners, Frank was motivated more by a desire to
provide a community focus than by profit-making and the
working class custom was never discouraged as it was
elsewhere. He also saw the success of both places in terms of
breaking down island differences and rivalries amongst West
Indians: he was Trinidadian but the Rio and the Mangrove
were West Indian. Frank described the atmosphere and
clientele like this:

> The coffee bar was open all night. Out of the Rio came many
> things – it was a kind of school, a 'university'. It just happened. It
> got a lot of hustlers, and it attracted West Indians from all the
> islands – from Jamaica, from Trinidad, from Barbados ... It
> attracted people who were rebellious and a bit smart, people with
> street intelligence, people for whom the British way of life, which
> was still coming to terms with working alongside black people,
> was full of subtle and blatant racism. This left the young and
> ambitious to look for a more compatible, self-determining
> life-style.

When Frank closed the Rio and moved on to the Mangrove,
it wasn't long before he had to accept that his ideal of a caring,
friendly community centre which offered a positive resource to
the community as a whole, was in fact acquiring another
unplanned dimension. The Mangrove became a place where
young black people sought refuge and collective defence
from the harassment on the streets outside. Uninterested in
trade unions or party politics, Frank found himself in the
position of a political leader, in the broadest sense of the word
'political', constantly engaged in local diplomacy and
negotiations. 'Organisation was needed,' he says, 'and
someone had to stick their neck out.'

He gradually acquired an ambiguous and difficult role within the community. On the one hand, he became one of the chief targets of the police, who believed him to be behind a whole range of illegal activity, from prostitution to gambling to drug-dealing. On the other, he was the buffer between the police and the black community, with the police tacitly acknowledging that his leadership had to be negotiated with and could assist them in controlling the community, whilst the youngsters turned to him for help in their rough dealings with the police.

The Mangrove was subjected to three police raids, on suspicion of drug offences, within months of opening. The third of these, in May 1970, fruitless as the first two, was the last straw for the Mangrove community who decided to organise a public protest against continuous police harassment in the Notting Hill area generally. On 9 August, a demonstration of about 300 people set off from outside the restaurant, intending to march past the three local police stations. Violent clashes with the police resulted in nine people being charged with riot, conspiracy, affray and assault. Along with Frank Crichlow, the Nine included Barbara Beese, Rupert Boyce, Rhodan Gordon, Darcus Howe, Antony Innes, Roddy Kentish, Althea Lecointe and Geoffrey Millet.

The trial, which took place towards the end of 1971 in the Old Bailey and lasted ten weeks, resulted in the acquittal of all defendants on the riot charges, although they received suspended sentences for more minor offences. For a massively political trial, it received comparatively little publicity in the national press, although amongst the black community nationally it was the focus of well-organised publicity and solidarity and seen as a watershed in the development of black self-organisation. The charade of nine articulate black people – three of whom conducted their own defence – confronting a white judge and court produced some memorable exchanges and incidents. Above all, it resulted in the total humiliation of the police whose flimsy, fabricated and conflicting evidence did them no credit. They could not even successfully distinguish between the two women defendants: all blacks looked the same to them, of course. Their allegation that the Mangrove was the haunt of 'criminals, prostitutes, ponces and the like' and that 'anyone who ended up there would be depraved and corrupt' looked very stupid alongside the string of character witnesses produced to give evidence for Frank Crichlow, including the local MP Bruce Douglas Mann, C.L.R. James, Lord Gifford, actress Vanessa Redgrave and writer Colin McInnes.

The trial judge resisted all efforts by the defendants and their lawyers (who were black and white) to have the court acknowledge and take into account the race dimension of the case. An unsuccessful attempt was made to secure an all-black jury, on the grounds that a fair trial needed to be conducted by their peers. In the end, only two of the jury members were black, though the defence successfully challenged and eliminated 63 potential jurors out of 100 offered to them. The gulf between judge and accused was most strikingly summed up by Darcus Howe, who said, 'The Judge says he has 35 years of legal experience. Well, I have 400 years of colonial experience.'

Barbara Beese, commenting now on the experience of the Mangrove Nine trial and its impact on black politics, says:

> It was a lesson in self-organisation for the black community. We learned that we couldn't rely on other people. We had to develop skills for ourselves. It's important for young activists today to be informed by that period. If they aren't, they risk being swallowed up by cultural nationalism.

Community Leadership

One of the reasons Frank Crichlow is seen as such as threat by the establishment, particularly the police, is that he is inseparable from his community. Darcus Howe said during the Mangrove trial that the Mangrove did not belong to Frank, it belonged to the whole West Indian community. Frank would go along with that; indeed, the statement represents the achievement of what he set out to create. But he is not the kind of community leader with whom the authorities feel comfortable, because he makes no concessions to their values. He isn't paid to represent his community but it – or sections of it, at least – can speak through him.

This is a qualitatively different role from the one played by the growing number of 'race professionals' in the community, whose jobs were created in the bodies set up by the series of Race Relations Acts in 1965, 1968 and 1976. The local 'conciliation committees' which came out of the 1965 Act gave way in 1968 to the Community Relations Commission. The 1976 Act then replaced the RRB and the CRC with the Commission for Racial Equality and the network of Community Relations Councils.

The posts which went with these organisations have always been seen in conflicting ways by the black community. Firstly, many of the jobs were occupied by white people, who knew how to operate within the system, but who could not possibly bring a black perspective with them even if they were suitably anti-racist in their outlook and sympathies. Opportunities were also created, however, for black people to move into professional jobs and this cannot easily be dismissed as a negligible development, even if it was largely tokenistic. The risk was that they were going to become removed from their communities and lose touch with the people whose interests they were meant to represent, in the context of a law which was hardly a watertight response to dealing with racism in the first place and towards which many of us felt deep suspicion. Not surprisingly, this was easily interpreted by many in the black community as a deliberate strategy by the state to weaken its growing sense of self-organisation and unity. (After all, the same thing had happened in the United States, epitomised in 1969 when the Ford Foundation funded and staged a conference on Black Power.)

I never felt the Race Relations Acts had much to offer us. Once I had got involved with the trade union movement I realised that the courts worked against the interests of working people, like the Industrial Relations Act in the early 1970s. So I had no faith in the Race Relations Act. I just saw black militants being creamed off to work at the Race Relations Board and the Community Relations Councils.

We were getting on fine. We were beginning to beat the system by ourselves. We could defend ourselves when attacked by the police. We brought over Cheddi Jagan, Stokely Carmichael, Bob Marley. Then we had Race Relations Acts. But to use them, you had to put yourself in jeopardy.

I would argue that the jobs in the so-called 'race relations industry' are both necessary and appropriate to the stage of development we have reached in British political life. The crucial thing for the black race professionals to remember is that their destiny as individuals lies with the destiny of the whole black community. An individual black perspective is not enough. A community black perspective is what counts, is what protects you from forgetting your tokenistic status and is what keeps you moving on the side of real progress rather than patching up the cracks. Experienced people like Asquith Gibbes, the senior community relations officer in Lewisham, Pansy Jeffries from Ladbroke Grove CAB, Winston Best, a teacher then later an inspector for multi-ethnic education in inner London, and many others, may have their smart clothes for work, their salaries and brief cases, but their first allegiance is to their community. The job might have middle-class status, but no matter what the Registrar General says, the individuals do not. The strength of black people in the 'race industry' jobs comes from the community, and their effectiveness depends on continuing to share that community's values. In the minds of white society, the black professionals are still freaks. All of us have heard phrases like, 'If only they were all like you,' or, 'We don't mind you, it's the others who are a problem,' so often it's like a family joke. The temptation to 'play white' is pressing, especially in a situation where you are numerically isolated. But to fall into that trap would not only weaken the individual's position, but weaken the community to whom he or she should remain answerable.

Despite the general scepticism towards the anti-discrimination legislation felt within the black community, the

1976 Act represented a significant advance over the previous two in that the concept of 'indirect discrimination' was included and made unlawful. Modelled on the Sex Discrimination Act 1975 and owing a great deal to the influence of the legal strategies being developed in the USA for both women's and black rights, the latest Race Relations Act also gave individuals the power to make a complaint for the first time. The political atmosphere into which it was introduced also differed significantly from the previous two. This time, it did not go hand in hand with further restrictions on immigration and so was able to be seen as more of a genuine progressive development, rather than 'an appeasement to the black community', as one black activist described its two predecessors.

It would be as big a mistake for the black community to dismiss wholesale the 1976 Act as yet another sop from the Labour government as it would for the government and the progressive white organisations and individuals who lobbied for the Act to ignore the role of the black community in shifting the conventional wisdom surrounding 'race relations' and the type of legislation that was needed. It was the tenacity of the black community itself, through its organisations, together with its direct experience and understanding of how racism works which led to the acceptance of the view that 'indirect' or 'institutional' discrimination had to be tackled.

The report on the West Indian community by the Select Committee on Race Relations and Immigration of its work during 1976 was published at the beginning of 1977, shortly after the new Act had been enforced.[11] It provides a useful expression of the turning point marked by the 1976 Act. Dozens of nationally and community based West Indian organisations had given evidence to the Select Committee, both orally and in writing, commenting in particular on the operation of the 1968 Act. There can be no doubt that the unity of West Indian opinion influenced the terms of the 1976 Act, in particular the inclusion of indirect discrimination and the new, positive statutory duty on local authorities to 'promote equality of opportunity' as well as the existing obligation to eliminate unlawful discrimination, the scope of which was considerably widened.

It must be said that parts of the Select Committee's report, not surprisingly, reflect prejudice and ignorance. For example, the West Indian family is still seen as inadequate: '... the family as the basic unit of security has been weakened and the generation gap, in fact, is more disruptive among West Indian than among any other families'.

This view seems to have been compounded by an extremely illogical, racist and sexist perception of family life in the West Indies itself, which the Committee visited as part of its programme of work. Commenting on how important it is for people in Britain to understand the structure of family life in the West Indies if misunderstandings are to be avoided, the report goes on to describe that structure which, of course, is different in many respects from the family structure of which the Select Committee members were part. The comparison is clearly, but totally tacitly, made. The give-away is that the patterns of family life, childbearing, childrearing and sexual experience, which to West Indians are normal are char-acterised here with the repeated use of the word 'instability'. Fundamental to the perceived instability, it appears, is that,

> the man's authority passes to the women and the role of the mother and grandmother is by far the strongest in the West Indian family system. Women from an early age are used to managing their own lives and to leaving their children in the care of others.

Sound quite stable to me.

The report also falls prey to the notion that West Indians, particularly the young, need *help* to develop certain qualities which are, in fact, precisely the qualities that had given us the strength to survive so far in such a hostile society. The report talks of the need to 'foster community organisation and self-reliance. The West Indian community is more in need than any other ethnic community.' Of the 'young West Indians born in this country', the report observes rather insensitively: 'They have not experienced the necessity for self-reliance and resourcefulness that, to a greater degree or less, all immigrants feel.'

However, a report written by white people for white people is not the place to look for a black perspective. Despite the pitfalls mentioned above, the reports very usefully set out what amounted to an agenda – *as defined by the black community* – of the areas of inequalities and discrimination which needed to be addressed and which the 1976 Act now equipped – indeed compelled – those in power to tackle, be they employers, local authorities, the media or public bodies. The tone of the report is acknowledged as coming from the community: '... the West Indian community have made it clear that they are looking for, and need, more than a sympathetic understanding of their problems and difficulties: they expect, and are entitled to expect, positive and effective action.'

Should any reader of this Select Committee report have been in doubt that inequalities existed, hard facts summarised the situation in a number of fields including housing, employment, unemployment, education and training. Although, for example, the level of owner-occupation was the same in the West Indian community as it was for the white population (50 per cent), access to council housing was still low and slow. Further, 34 per cent of West Indian households were reported to be living at a density of two or more people per bedroom, compared with only 11 per cent of white households. Unemployment was considerably higher than the national average within the West Indian community and for those in work average earnings were lower. Inadequate provision for the under-fives is heavily flagged up as needing attention and action, as is the need for more black teachers. The emphasis on education and opportunities for the young reflects the nature of the West Indian community's population structure. The 1971 census showed that a much greater proportion of our community was under 25 years old than in the population as a whole or than in other 'immigrant' groups. Over half our community was under fifteen: more than double the national figure.

One of the themes touched on by the report and which sets the scene for the period from 1976 which is analysed in the next chapter is the democratic participation of the black community in society. The Runnymede Trust had pointed in its evidence to the very small numbers of black magistrates, councillors, school governors and others holding public office. At the time, Lambeth and Brent each had two West Indian councillors; Haringey had one. On its visit to Sheffield, the Select Committee was told that 'there had never been a West Indian member of the local education committee or indeed any similar committee'. The West Indian Standing Conference told the Committee that 'through the whole strata of the democratic organisation in Great Britain, we should be able to see persons in positions of authority,' and this submission was 'fully accepted' by the Committee. However, in the words of the report, 'Democracy works by majority but it is not just a question of numbers.' The writers of the report most probably did not appreciate the full significance of the remark. It makes a very good opening to the third – and current – stage of this account of the West Indian contribution to British social and political life, in which our struggle for equality challenges the concept of democracy: not to defeat it, but to extend it.

Notes

1. House of Commons *Hansard*, 6 December 1973, Vol. 865.
2. F. Dhondy, B. Beese and L. Hassan, *The Black Explosion in British Schools*, Race Today Publications, 1982.
3. *The Education of Immigrants*, DES Circular, 7/65, London, June 1965.
4. M. Maxwell, 'Violence in the Toilets', *Race Today*, Vol. 1, No. 5, September 1969.
5. National Council for Commonwealth Immigrants, *The Education of West Indian Immigrant Children*, London, 1968.
6. Dhondy *et al.*, op. cit.
7. B. Coard, *How the West Indian Child is Made Educationally Sub-normal in the British School System*, New Beacon Books, 1971.
8. S. Delsol, *Supplementary Schools*, November 1984.
9. M. Stone, *The Education of the Black Child in Britain*, Fontana, 1981.
10. House of Commons *Hansard*, 6 December 1973, vol. 865.
11. Select Committee on Race Relations and Immigration, *The West Indian Community*, Vol. 1, Session 1976-7, HMSO, 1977.

5   The Fight For Equality

The relationship between the left and black people is like the relationship between parent and child. They always know what's best for us. But now, black people are moving too fast for the left.

Challenging institutional racism has to be done within the context of aiming to change the whole social order. In order words, with a socialist objective.

Most political commentators on the left have seen the election of the Thatcher government in 1979 as the turning point heralding a new political era both for British society in general and for the left. This does not altogether reflect the black experience. Whilst the policies of Mrs Thatcher's government have indeed been shaped by economic theories and moral values which have delivered decisive blows to the quality of life, choices and expectations of the majority of the British people, the savagery of the resulting inequalities is not something to which black people found themselves exposed only from 1979. Our analysis of inequality, as the last chapter illustrated, underpinned the campaign for the 1976 Race Relations Act. You could say that the black community had a head-start of three years over the rest of the left in the battle against Thatcherism. Yet it took Thatcher's defeat of Labour to drive the left into its first serious examination of the identity and whereabouts of the working class and to accept that it was not only white and male. It also discovered that it was no longer blindly loyal to Labour.

The formal, though belated, acknowledgement of black people as part of the working class, however, is no guarantee at all that the racism we suffer has also been adequately acknowledged. Racism cannot be dealt with solely within the

framework of class politics. The assumption of a natural
alliance between the organised working class and black people,
although traditionally held by people in both groups, has
borne fruit only in a limited and sporadic way; in general, the
past three or four decades have seen little involvement by the
labour and trade union movement in the main concerns of
black people. And the extent to which black people have
participated in the key struggles of trade unionism, for
example, has largely been either ignored (such as in the health
workers' dispute) or glorified as if it marked a great new
dawning of consciousness on the part of *black* people, rather
than white people's perception of black people (such as in the
Grunwick dispute).

The interests of the working class movement and the black
movement do coincide, given that both lay claim to their fair
share of material power and wealth, which would entail a
massive redistribution of both. But since the vast majority of
black people in Britain are also of the working class, and
amongst its poorest members, redistribution within the class is
also required if a genuinely democratic outcome is to be
achieved. (The women's movement has advanced the same
argument in respect of redistribution of wealth between the
sexes.) The unity of class interests can be shattered when white
working people are faced with demands from the black
community for, say, a proportion of seats on a trade union
executive committee, or a restructuring of local authority
policy on housing allocation to give more and better housing
to black people. In other words, for black people to be treated
fairly and democratically and not to be discriminated against
because of our colour, some of the power and material assets
which need to be transferred must come from the white
working class.

The alliance, therefore, is only 'natural' up to a point,
assuming the ideology and practice of both member-groups of
that alliance are unchanging and unchangeable. But to make
that assumption would be to fall for a mechanical and
monolithic approach to political change. And dead-end
politics will achieve nothing. What I am trying to show is that

the struggles of the black community are acting as a catalyst for wider changes in both the structure and attitudes of the working class as a whole. Some shifts have already been noticeable and notable; the potential is far greater. This chapter brings the black struggle up to date and shows how its vision has developed from a purely anti-racist perspective to one which is also increasingly conscious of being pro-equality and pro-democracy.

The emphasis on education as an arena of black struggle is significant. As the opening chapters testified, the promise of education drew West Indians to Britain in the first place. We knew that education helps to determine people's future. Our community's involvement in campaigns on educational provision and content has also been to do with giving our people a past, one with which we could identify and which we could feel proud of. The fight for a good education for black children, however, has opened the door to a far wider debate on what a good education is for all children, about who should determine its content and who should control its delivery and administration. It is fair to question whether an initiative from any other section of the working class on education matters could be taken without the lead from the campaigns originating in the black community, or without reference to them.

Our alienation from mainstream society and our determination to achieve equality has led to two forms of positive resistance: on the streets and in institutions. The way in which black street politics have developed owes much to the historical neglect by the labour movement of the black experience.

The working class disillusion with Labour in the few years leading up to the 1979 General Election in which Mrs Thatcher triumphed had an important impact on the experience of black people and the continued rise of popular racism.

Increasing unemployment, together with the public-spending cuts implemented by the Labour government and the failure of inner-city, Labour-controlled local authorities to deliver the goods in housing, social services and education, created a frustration which many found difficult and uncomfortable to articulate. How could they blame the people's party when they were the people? The National Front and similar organisations provided an easier alternative: blame the blacks. A number of by-elections gave the NF a chance to rally significant new areas of support, particularly amongst young people. This line of attack was, of course, old hat to the black community. But the white left seemed puzzled and slow in its response. It was not until 1977 that the Anti-Nazi League was formed, a whole decade after the NF had unleashed itself onto the political scene. There had been anti-fascist activity before 1977, but it took time for the connections to be made between anti-Semitism and racism. The ANL was established after the gruesome confrontation which occurred during an NF demonstration in New Cross, Lewisham, an area with a large black population. The Home Secretary had resisted a campaign to ban the NF's provocative march and the violent clashes were inevitable, police tactics not being as clear-cut as they became on subsequent occasions.

Although in the black community up to 1977 we felt we were very much on our own against racist abuse and attack, without any appreciable support from the left and the labour movement, the nature of the Anti-Nazi League was not exactly the kind of solidarity we had hoped for and the response to it was cynical and distanced. The emphasis on being anti-Nazi as opposed to anti-racist, although the former was supposed to embrace the latter, signalled to us that here again was another white organisation which, in its attempt to be broad-based had overlooked the perspective, needs and demands of our community. The ANL's inaugural meeting was held in the House of Commons. I was invited along to be '*the* black activist' (my emphasis) on the committee. I declined, saying this was obviously white people's business.

The League based its appeal on the threat of the NF to democracy, not to black people, even though the main focus of NF propaganda was anti-black and in celebration of racism. Older activists from the black community, rooted as we were in the labour movement, could not identify with the ANL's apparent reluctance to work with the traditional labour movement structures, notwithstanding the racism we knew to be there too. The younger activists, by and large, also had problems dealing with the ANL.

> The left is as bad as, if not worse than, the right as far as race is concerned. What went on during the planning for the demonstration against the National Front in Haringey in 1977 shocked black people. Some young West Indians wanted to organise physical confrontation. We wanted to include them in the overall planning, otherwise we could see they would go their own way and there would be trouble. But the white left wouldn't accommodate them at all. They just wanted to dictate everything and keep things under their control. No dialogue was possible. This happened all the time with the All London Campaign against Racism and Fascism. The same with the Anti-Nazi League.

Once again, we turned to self-help and self-reliance, qualities ironically amongst those which Mrs Thatcher professed to value and wish to see develop in order to relieve the state of its over-burdened responsibilities. Unfortunately for Mrs Thatcher, our idea of self-reliance rested on a consolidation of our collective black identity, which conflicted with her emphasis on individual self-sufficiency and competitiveness. Our resourcefulness was a *challenge* to the inequality we faced, a bid for a bigger cake and an equal share of it. What Thatcherism meant by 'self-help' amounted to an *acceptance* of inequality.

Criminalising Resistance

Although 1976 was the year in which the new Race Relations Act held some promise of assisting in the dismantling of institutional racism, it was the Notting Hill Carnival of that year which turned out to be a more realistic symbol of the end of the period during which the state hoped to achieve 'harmonious race relations' by getting white people to respect our 'cultural diversity'. Unable to cope with an event which had a specific cultural and political significance for West Indians, which had grown organisationally into a continuous all-year-round project and which provided the black community with a unique opportunity for self-expression, defiance of authority and internal solidarity, the police decided it had to be contained, controlled, moved, or preferably banned. In 1975, the Carnival had been policed by 80 officers. In 1976, no fewer than 1,600 were deployed. Cecil Gutzmore described the outcome in an article published in *Marxism Today*:

> The police, who felt they had large enough forces to withstand anything, moved without restraint. They claimed to be making arrests of pickpockets. In reality they were laying into black youths with truncheons and a certain abandon. The youths fought back. The battle spread to envelop large areas of the part of Notting Hill known locally as The Grove. Hundreds of youths joined battle against the blatantly misused police power which is in reality part of the daily experience of the black community as a whole. It was a terrain brimming over with missiles, with bricks, half bricks, bottles and canned soft drinks ... Pictures of these battles went round the world, once more giving Notting Hill the notoriety it had not experienced since 1958, the year of its historic race riots. The battle of the 1976 Notting Hill Carnival gave world-wide confirmation to the fact that the culture of the black communities in the UK is inescapably one of resistance.[1]

The following year at Carnival, the police arrived with riot shields. But their harassment did not just occur at annual intervals. It persisted week in week out at the expense of the black community in the area, with Frank Crichlow and All Saints Road amongst the persistent targets. Frank was on bail continuously for ten years, from 1970 to 1980, on a series of charges not a single one of which resulted in his conviction. Crime statistics continued to be distorted by the media, to the extent that the whole black community felt it had been criminalised on sight. The celebrated Mangrove Nine were succeeded in the courts by the Islington 18 in 1977 and the Lewisham 21 in 1978. The Asian communities too were the butt of increasing police attention: the whole Asian community in Southall was turned on by the police in 1979, when the National Front demonstrated through their streets.

Blair Peach died at police hands in their attempt to 'protect' the NF's freedom to march.

The impact of black criminalisation was not confined to the men and boys. Three young black women interviewed in *Spare Rib* magazine described the effect on them too: 'It's like they're trying to say that every single Black person out there, man, woman or child, is a criminal. Since those reports I've had looks from white people.' Another said: 'Like when I went to sit down in a bus, and a white woman grabbed her bag. I felt awful.'[2] Meanwhile, 'the leafier parts of Kensington', as one *Time Out* journalist put it, 'seem to be able to party and double-park and hooray-henry till the early hours without the police having to act on quite so many tip-offs.'

Schools were not immune to police harassment either. One school in North London was taken completely by surprise one day to see several police officers land in the playground in a *helicopter*.

An invasion of the school where I taught in East London took place one day in 1979 when I was on playground duty. A boy drew my attention to two police officers, whom I approached to find out what they wanted. As I turned round, I couldn't believe my eyes. Climbing over the school wall were another five or six policemen. My polite questions went completely unanswered. When I demanded a reply, I got a one-finger salute from one of the guardians of the peace. All of this was in full view of about 200 boys. Finally I got through to the sergeant who said a woman had made a complaint that a lad had exposed himself to her. When I asked why, in that case, his men were in the process of searching two boys and having them empty their pockets, and pointed out that one was black and the other white, the sergeant got the point and turned purple. By this time the headmaster had been summoned. He also got very short shrift. It was very embarrassing for him to be humiliated in the playground in front of his own pupils. He had the consolation, however, of the total sympathy of all the kids.

There was a sting in the tail for the police over this whole episode which also gave us some satisfaction. We made a complaint, of course, and discovered the support of one witness we had not known had observed the entire charade: the local beat policeman. He too complained to his seniors that in fifteen minutes those six officers had undone about eighteen months of painstaking work he had done trying to build bridges with the school's staff and pupils.

The young came under attack again in Bristol in 1980, when the police raided one of their local meeting places, the ironically named Black and White Cafe. When Frank Crichlow was invited to Bristol afterwards to discuss the events and subsequent criminal proceedings with parents and community leaders, his every move between London and Bristol was followed and monitored by the police, presumably hoping to uncover some murky conspiracy. The forces of 'law and order', however, once again failed to convict anyone on riot charges.

Brixton became the next major flashpoint in 1981. In February 1981 Lambeth Council had published the report of an enquiry into local police-community relations, which described local policing as 'an army of occupation'. One month later, major riots broke out. Further resistance in July 1981 sparked off similar rebellion in at least 25 other cities and towns. Like Notting Hill, the Brixton area had lived through years of relentless police harassment and abuse of powers. The Scarman enquiry following the uprising conceded the existence of racist attitudes amongst the police, but provocatively, unintelligently and insultingly rejected the presence of institutional racism, whilst at the same time validating the police's corruption of statistics to produce black criminality.

By the end of 1985, the diversion of some central Government funds into inner-city projects to keep black youth off the streets, plus a few courses in racism awareness for the police, had predictably not proved a sufficient response to prevent another uprising in Brixton and the addition of Liverpool 8, Handsworth and Tottenham to the roll call of battlegrounds between the black community and the police. Shortly after the Handsworth 'riot', the West Indian Standing Conference resolved to conduct enquiries and consultations with its affiliated bodies and other community leaders in the

Birmingham area. What we found out confirmed once more that the 'riot' in no way could be put down to spontaneous criminal activity by individual black youths. The events were totally predictable and firmly within the context of prolonged police harassment and general racism from the white community towards a black population overwhelmed by the futility of unemployment.

Several days before the rebellion, there had been a meeting of about 300 people under the aegis of the Residents' Association for the Handsworth district. Nearly three-quarters of those present were white and included the Lord Mayor, local MPs and senior police officers. The meeting had been preceded, in the words of one black community activist, by 'some of the most horrendous police raids that we had in the district of Handsworth, under the pretext that they were cracking down on drugs'. He went on:

> Some of the most racist statements were made and, at one stage, a member of the police threatened that they would be prepared to shoot people. Also what was mentioned in the meeting was that the Residents' Association were now prepared to establish vigilante groups. So the word went out that everybody should be careful because there was going to be a spate of racial attacks in the district again.[3]

Neither the black community nor the white left and labour movement has yet analysed the situation adequately enough to formulate a political response to black inner-city rebellion, or to work out whether their interests in such politics share anything in common. Part of the framework for an analysis must be optimism. Both youth and numbers are on our side. Secondly, the inner-city rebellion must be interpreted as a positive development, from an historical perspective, despite the level of violence which has included the tragic deaths of both black and white people. For the white left, being positive about black rebellion means avoiding the trap of response and interpretation in terms of civil liberties and police accountability before racism and institutional discrimination; in other words, the organised left needs much more

convincingly to accept that, for once, it is not centre-stage on
this issue and that the actual experience of black people must
determine any political analysis and consequent political
action. For the sections of the black community not directly
involved on the streets – which means, by and large, the older
generation, the middle class and the younger people who may
have come from the streets but are now cushioned by decently
paid jobs in the 'race industry' – thinking positive has to mean
acknowledging that the ones on the streets are struggling in the
only form available to them. They may not use terminology
like 'institutional racism', but they are an undeniable part of
the same battle which some of us have the opportunity to wage
professionally. When they get busted, others get promoted.

A good example of the direct positive impact of the street
rebellions on local authority policies occurred over the
summer of 1981. In June, the Rampton report on the
education of children from West Indian families was
published, strongly identifying institutional racism as the main
factor leading to black under-achievement in schools (and to
which I shall return later). One of Rampton's recommendations was that all local education authorities should have
policies on multi-ethnic and anti-racist education. At the time,
you didn't need all the fingers on one hand to count the
number of Local Education Authorities which already had
such policies. During that summer Brixton erupted. By the
beginning of the autumn term, nearly thirty LEAs were dotting
the i's and crossing the t's on their policies.

Street politics did not spring up from nowhere. The youth
may not have any conception of themselves as immigrants or
products of colonialism, but their struggle is a continuation of
the resistance which the immigrants of the fifties and sixties put
up first to colonialism at home, then to the racism with which
we were unexpectedly confronted in Britain. Our means of
resistance differ; our culture of resistance is the same.

The impact of international politics is one of the links of
resistance between the generations in the black community.
Earlier chapters have shown how the politics of the fifties
generation were shaped by our identification with the struggles

for national independence in the Caribbean and Africa. In the eighties, the activists in the front line have shown a similar identification with the black struggle in South Africa, even though their information stems on the whole from media coverage rather than political involvement. The connections between black oppression in South Africa and inner-city Britain should not be romanticised – the rule of apartheid is a different order of oppression altogether than the racism within a democracy, albeit an increasingly authoritarian democracy. Nevertheless, the scope for making political connections and acting in solidarity is a further cause for optimism. It cannot fail to be noticed that the government in Britain which has carried out policies to the detriment of inner-city areas is the same government which colludes with apartheid in southern Africa. These connections have produced a participation in traditional forms of political action amongst sections of the black community which otherwise operate wholly outside the reference points of the left; for example, the huge contingent on the demonstration against Botha's visit to Britain, which was mobilised by the Mangrove Community Association. And again on the Anti-Apartheid Movement's national demonstration in 1985, where significantly, Jesse Jackson was one of the main speakers. His presence not only broadened the appeal of the demonstration to the religious black community, but also symbolised the historical unity between black peoples in struggle across the world.

Mrs Thatcher and some of her government Ministers went to great lengths to dismiss the idea that unemployment and social deprivation were amongst the key root causes of the inner-city rebellions. The total lack of understanding by people who live in a different social and economic world from those who eke out a living on unemployment or supplementary benefit was illustrated in 1985 by the pathetic spectacle of Lord Gowrie who claimed he could not manage on his £30,000 a year salary as Minister for the Arts. But anecdotes aside, the Tory line that 'riots' are caused by unrepresentative criminals on the rampage is essentially an attempt to conceal two important features of the black struggle: first, that it arises out of a collective consciousness of our oppression and, secondly, that it is about power. Not power for the sake of it, or more power than anyone else, but the power of economic security denied by unemployment (not only to the black community), which would allow people more control over their own lives, and the power of an equal share of the services, resources and decision-making in society as a whole. The black community does not need to be accommodated in a paternalistic fashion, it needs to participate on the basis of equality. The structural denial of our right to participate and be empowered is what the term 'institutional racism' describes. The application of institutional racism was acknowledged first in the field of education, as Bernard Coard's pamphlet on West Indian children in ESN schools illustrated, although the phrase itself was not used at that time; similarly in Marina Maxwell's article, 'Violence in the Toilets', which had pointed to factors such as the inadequacy of teacher training and the school curriculum to cater for the needs of black children, thereby condemning them to failure.

Institutional Racism

When the Rampton Committee was conducting its enquiry, a visit to Rugby (the town, not the school) provided an example of hidden discrimination which achieved a breakthrough in the Committee members' understanding of the practice and effect of institutional racism. We, the Committee members, were simply looking at the way in which the boundaries were drawn for the catchment areas for certain schools with the best reputations. Black parents had been complaining that they could not get their children into these schools and felt dissatisfied with the explanation that it was not out of racist discrimination, just the effect of the catchment area. When matched up to the distribution of housing across ethnic groups, however, it was clearly revealed that black families lived on the wrong side of the dividing line. The impact of the interrelation of housing patterns and the education authority's catchment areas suddenly dawned on us all, Committee members, black

parents and white headteachers alike. Even without
intent, the system as a whole was discriminatory.

In housing too, studies in the seventies in London
that, despite the existence of black councillors and po
which proclaimed equality of opportunity, public hous
allocation still operated effectively in a racist way by attaching
priority to criteria which black people were less likely to meet,
such as residence qualifications.[4] Discrimination occurred even
if it was not intended or planned for. Indeed, it could often
result even if there was an explicit political will to apply fair
treatment.

Another example of the unconscious but nevertheless
systematic exclusion of black people's presence in an area of
social provision struck the black community in Hackney in
1980. Lloyd King, a Jamaican who had grown up in the
borough and was by then active in local community politics,
was a member of a group of teachers and others who were
interested in finding out whether the local libraries reflected
the whole community's needs. But when he enquired at his
local library for books and records by Paul Robeson, Lloyd
found that not only was Paul Robeson missing, but there was
absolutely nothing in stock relating to the West Indian or
Afro-Caribbean community. It was an area with a large Jewish
community and their history and culture was, quite rightly,
reflected in the material available in the public libraries. We
had to achieve the same recognition of our presence.

The issue was taken up with the Hackney Council for Racial
Equality and a campaign was set up seeking to democratise the
library service to reflect the true composition of the
community it served. The campaign met with the usual
bureaucratic resistance. No resources were available and there
was no policy about a multi-cultural or anti-racist approach to
services at the time. Lobbying council officers and holding
meetings got nowhere. So the campaign took itself to the Town
Hall, disrupted council meetings and staged a sit-in. The
politicians mouthed sympathetic noises but implored the
protestors not to use such visible methods; after all, they said,
they were our allies.

owever, knew the road to hell was
nd pressed their case regardless of
to the Labour councillors. In the
through Section 11 of the 1966
employ specialist librarians and
of years later, one of Hackney's
ed, after C.L.R. James, the
al. The Hackney campaign had
ional) repercussions, as other
.....ies acknowledged a role for themselves in the struggle
against racism, by providing appropriate materials and
effectively opening their doors to a broader section of the
community than before.

Institutional discrimination does not operate only against
black people, of course. The women's movement has long
campaigned over the neglect and exclusion of women and
discrimination against them in the whole construction of
society, its institutions and laws. Discrimination and
oppression on grounds of sex, race and class are all linked by
the experience of prejudice and powerlessness of their victims,
in a society where the ruling class is white and male. Which is
not to say that a unity of interests between the oppressed
groups is an automatic corollary to that shared experience. For
example, trade unions may be pro-working class, but they are
institutionally racist and sexist. And the women's movement
has consciously had to devote a great deal of effort and energy
into resisting domination by white women, whose priorities
have not always coincided with the issues of importance from a
black woman's perspective.

Both the women's rights and black rights lobbies, however,
shared the same fairly rapid disillusion with the impact of the
anti-discrimination laws on 1975 and 1976. Neither lobby had
believed that legal intervention alone would be the cure-all for
discrimination, particularly when the Acts contained loopholes
and compromises. But the scope of the law against indirect
discrimination and the sections permitting limited positive
action remain largely unexploited in both sex and race cases.
Obstacles to fair redress under the law were also predictably

encountered in the judicial system itself, including industrial tribunals, controlled as it is by white men. The success rate of Race Relations Act cases proved to be low. In 1982, out of 200 cases brought to industrial tribunals, only 30 were successful. This disincentive contributed to a decline in the number of cases brought forward in subsequent years.

The 1976 Race Relations Act, however, contains an important provision not present in the Sex Discrimination Act and that is the positive duty placed on local authorities to promote equality of opportunity. This reflects the pressure of the black community on Parliament during the early seventies, backed up by official statistics and research which confirmed the extent of social and economic inequality amongst black people. The advantage of this duty on local authorities is that it has given expression to the black community's *collective* state of disadvantage and provided opportunities for *collective* redress, as opposed to the need for an individual to pursue a complaint of direct or indirect discrimination. In other words, the concept of institutional racism had a framework within which it could be applied and followed through, using the law as a reference point which strengthened the legitimacy of campaigns to shift local authority policies and practices.

The fact that black people are a minority in Britain means that the challenge to institutional racism ultimately involves change which affects more than simply the interests of and benefits to black people. It involves a challenge to the way democracy operates, its mechanisms and its means of accountability. The process of dismantling institutional racism is not just about getting rid of something negative. It is about promoting new forms of organisation and decision-making, which are fair and representative given the composition of the society we live in. Screening out institutional racism will have an impact also on the power relationships between other groups.

Securing and extending democratic rights has always been of concern and priority to the left. What the left has failed to take into account over the last decade is that the areas of organised struggle on which the black community have focussed have been about democracy and not just racism in isolation. The failure to recognise this has helped to keep issues of racism on the margins of the left's agenda rather than in the centre of an analysis which acknowledges the lead given by the black community in pointing the left in a more constructive political direction. The achievements of the black community can ultimately lead to achievements for all people. The political role of the black community as a catalyst for change has been evident in inner-city local authority politics, particularly over education policies, and more recently, within the trade union movement and Labour Party. This is a period and a process which is far from complete. But from the standpoint of the mid-eighties, it is essential for both the black community and the white left to develop a clearer understanding of the contribution of the black struggle for equality to the political life of Britain, if the *whole* working class and democratic movement is to be able to go forward and shift society from the basis of inequality to one of genuine equality of opportunity for all.

From Multi-Culturalism to Anti-Racism

The education system is the clearest example of where the initiatives coming from the black community have shifted conventional wisdom and official policies about what constitutes good education for anyone, black or white.

The institutional response to the first wave of black protest over our children's failure at the hands of the education system between the mid-sixties and mid-seventies was the development by a number of LEAs of policies on 'multi-cultural education'. The political context was one of attempting to soften up the black community by showing tolerance and respect towards our cultural differences. In educational terms, this led to an approach which has aptly been caricatured as 'the three S's': saris, samosas and steel bands.

What was fundamentally inadequate about the 'multi-cultural' approach was firstly, that it had not escaped from measuring black culture against a white British norm, which therefore rendered anything else inferior. Secondly, no-one asked black parents what they wanted for their children. The few research studies which did, discovered an ambivalence amongst West Indian parents towards the promotion of black culture in their children's schools. As one parent said in a study conducted in Handsworth in 1979, 'There ain't no O level in black studies yet.'[5] Thirdly, multi-cultural education still left black children underachieving academically. The three S's addressed the fringes of educational life, but ignored the fundamentals such as low teacher expectation, which together with direct racism combined to channel black pupils into CSE classes instead of O level classes, for example; or, worse, to channel them onto the streets by a racist application of the rules on suspension and expulsion.

A formal investigation by the Commission for Racial Equality into the suspension procedures of Birmingham LEA between 1974 and 1980, which it took to be a representative picture of similar multi-racial urban areas, concluded that the complaints of black parents were well-founded and that there were a disproportionate number of black suspensions and referrals to special units.[6] Black pupils were found to be four times as likely as white pupils to be suspended from secondary schools, for the same reasons. Institutional racism was blamed and the local authority, observing its duty under the Race Relations Act, changed the procedures.

Rastafari is cited in the investigation report as one of the factors which contributed to the racist application of suspension procedures – particularly ironic given the climate of official encouragement to 'tolerate' cultural diversity. But the CRE commented:

Rastafari became a significant factor in some parts of the black community in the late 1970s. Teachers tended to perceive it as a threat to their authority and the orderliness of the classroom. Rastafarian culture, through belief, style of behaviour, appearance and dress, was at odds with most forms of school organisation and many teachers were sceptical of its integrity. Rastafari is revealed as a significant factor, especially for girls, where it was referred to in one in four cases of West Indian girls suspended compared to approximately one in eight cases of West Indian boys. References to Rastafari became manifest in the data through teachers' comments on the appearance, language and dress of West Indian pupils suspended.

Multi-culturalism without anti-racism simply tinkered around at the edges. Chris Mullard located multi-cultural education theoretically within the ideology of colonialism:

> The way in which a colonial society has always perceived itself and its historical role in the development of capitalism and western civilisation suddenly but quite logically manifested itself in its identification of the problem as a *black problem*. As we can see from the very first policy statement of any long-lasting significance, it was a response that was embedded in the notion that the social order and its assumed unitary value system needed to be protected at all costs.[7]

The shortcomings of the multi-cultural approach left the black community continuing to draw on its own reserves and resourcefulness to supplement their children's education. Supplementary schools increasingly plugged the gap between parents' expectations of the system and its reality. An Association of Black Supplementary Schools was formed, which held a conference in February 1982 to assess the movement's development and shape its future. As the number of schools has grown and both local authorities and mainstream schools have begun to recognise their contribution, the nature of the relationship between the community schools and the authorities has in some cases become problematic. On the one hand, black parents and teachers want and need official support in terms of recognition and financial assistance for their work in supplementary education, but ways of achieving this without the authority turning its support into interference are sometimes difficult to develop. Some activists would sound loud warning bells:

> I'm worried that the supplementary school movement has been colonised by the state. Having access to grants has lost us our independence and autonomy. I'm suspicious of strings being

attached – a certain level of attendance, this or that on the curriculum. In the early days the struggle to keep the school alive financially was an important focus for community development and involvement, and for keeping up front the concerns of the black community about the education of our children. With state funding we could lose that involvement and that talent. A different type of person is thrown up: the ones who are good at presenting grant-aid proposals, but who may lack exposure to that all-important early experience, or who may even not be aware of it. It's too easy to sit back and not bother with the consciousness-raising any more, with the result that our supplementary schools become passive rather than active instruments for change.

The dangers anticipated in this statement by an activist in the Inner London area may seem like luxurious worries to the black community in areas where local authority grants to supplementary schools are still a pipe-dream and jumble sales are still the fund-raising order of the day. But it is as well to strengthen our conviction sooner rather than later that supplementary schools must remain the property of the community. The greater the participation, the less likely it will be that a local authority, with or without a grant to offer, will be able to 'colonise' them.

The evidence given by black community groups running supplementary schools was a crucial component in determining the findings of the Rampton Committee which reported in 1981 and pointed the education system away from narrow multi-culturalism alone, towards anti-racism.[8] This report was an interim report leading eventually to the Swann Report in 1985 which covered the education of a number of ethnic minority communities in addition to West Indian.[9] By 1975, as we have seen in the last chapter, the Labour Government realised that the black community was a force to be reckoned with when it came to education. The Select Committee on Immigration and Race Relations recommended that an enquiry be held into the education of West Indian children. Events on the part of the government were not exactly speedy, despite the obvious recognition that the black community was on the move and the old chestnut of blaming the black family and the IQs of black children were being more and more powerfully resisted. A DES consultative document in 1977 eventually led to the establishment of the Rampton/-Swann Committee. I was one of the four West Indians invited to serve on the Committee.

The Rampton Committee spent the first six months feeling around the issues. It was a frustrating time for the few black members; many of our white colleagues had next to no appreciation of the racism issue, but, gradually, their perspectives shifted. The verbal evidence in particular which we received helped to convince them that racism was at the top of black people's priorities.

The four West Indian members were wary, being in a minority and approaching the subject with a completely different life experience from the white majority. Although I was nominated as an individual, I felt that the invitation to join acknowledged my role as a community activist as well as a black teacher. I was therefore conscious throughout that not only did I have the duty to provide a community perspective, but also be accountable to the community for my role on the committee and for its findings. From my perspective of having lived in a colonialist society, I was aware that the function of a committee of enquiry could often serve to confuse people, stave off confrontation or misdirect the issues. We, the West Indians, had therefore to devise a method of operation as committee members which related to the wider black community. With funding from the Caribbean Teachers' Association, we travelled up and down the country, talking to people in the black community, asking for their support and discussing the issues. They understood that we recognised – and shared – their cynicism towards government enquiries. But they also understood that their support could strengthen our position on the commitee and influence the outcome. On the whole, we won that support.

The Rampton Report was published in 1981, the year of the so-called inner-city riots. Racism emerged clearly as the key factor behind West Indian 'under-achievement'. The high

profile given to racism caused a furore, in both the media and
government (by then Conservative). Antony Rampton himself
was asked to resign by the Secretary of State for Education.
Some of the Committee members, including me, were in no
doubt that his 'sacking' was precipitated by the strong line on
racism taken in the report. The report was a major victory for
the black members of the committee (including those from the
Asian communities) – and some of our white colleagues – who
had fought hard to win this particular ideological battle. Some
other committee members had been hell-bent on blaming the
black family for abdicating its responsibility towards its
children. They lost that position completely. An editorial in the
Times Educational Supplement which suggested that the 'West
Indian tail wagged the Rampton dog' was a recognition that
our presence on the committee had indeed been effective.

After Rampton, the Conservative government was not
enthusiastic about continuing with the enquiry. In the event, it
was persuaded, but under the new chairmanship of Lord
Swann, who very clearly did not share the same interest in the
issue as his predecessor. His perspective was governed by a
desire to dilute the racism factor, expressed by his two main
concerns at the outset of his term of office. First, if racism were
to blame, his question was why did Asian children achieve
better than West Indians, when both groups suffered racism
and the Asians had an even worse experience of racial
harassment? Secondly, there was an attempt to resuscitate the
black family as partly responsible for West Indian under-
achievement, as part of a retreat from the analysis based on
institutional racism.

In the event, the final report represented a significant
advance. The interim findings from the Rampton Report were
confirmed: racism, both in the system itself and on the part of
individuals' attitudes, was held to account for the 'failure' of
black children. Swann went even further. Added to racism, the
social and economic disadvantage of the whole working class,
which includes the vast majority of black people in Britain, was
identified as determining our 'failure'. The report of a major,
government-appointed enquiry confirmed what the black

community had said all along. The West Indians were in a minority of four; we won on some issues debated and naturally we lost on some too. The report has its weaknesses, for example its failure to explain the colonialist roots of racism. But on the crucial issue of the cause of so-called West Indian under-achievement, the committee successfully put paid to any possibility of teachers, LEAs, researchers or governments ever again explaining the academic failure of our children as a result of inferior IQs or inadequate family life. And in bringing together race *and* class in its analysis, Swann opened up wider possibilities for pressurising the system to change.

Swann has been criticised for saying nothing new and for being racist. But that is to misunderstand the function of such a report. For it to have confirmed the black community's views on education, and repeat our demands as recommendations, is something of a victory in itself. More black teachers, anti-racist policies for schools, more access courses and with mandatory grants, proper teacher training for education in a multi-cultural society, dealing with 'all-white' schools as well as those attended by black children, to name only a few, are some of these recommendations. But the real point is that all these things are now being said to the policy makers and practioners themselves. Swann is not addressed to the black community. We never needed it: we knew it already. But we live in the real world and in a racist society. So we have to acknowledge that the authority of our experience is not the same as the authority of an official enquiry's findings.

From the moment Swann was published, the reaction of the government, if nothing else, indicated that the report had, by and large, got it right. The government did its best to restrict media coverage of and popular interest in the report by bringing out another major education document only two days later. Secretary of State for Education, Sir Keith Joseph, more or less disowned the report in a statement from the House of Commons. He certainly made it clear that no more money would be forthcoming to do as the report recommended. A strong set of proposals, designed to correct the failings of the whole education system and help it not only to work for black children, but also to provide a better education for *all* children, was an embarrassment to a government openly committed to the opposite of equality of opportunity and an expansion of public expenditure.

The title of the Swann Report is *Education for All*, reflecting the committee's view that a multi-cultural *and* anti-racist education is appropriate for all children, not just black children. Indeed, the need for such a perspective to govern the education in schools where there are few or no black children could be said to be the most urgent. The report rejects the old ideas of assimilation and integration of the black and ethnic minority communities within a white 'norm', and instead emphasises the pluralist nature of society today, which the education system has so far failed to accept or reflect.

In the wake of Swann, however, the question of whether or not the black community and the rest of the organised working class can build the alliance for change which the *implementation* of Swann requires, has become more urgent a question to address than ever. For while Swann speaks of a pluralist society and we talk of democratisation, the DES has a very different direction in mind. An internal discussion document revealed in a research study in 1984 by Stewart Ranson indicates that the educational aspirations of those oppressed by class and/or race have a hurdle rather larger than the Swann Report to tackle.[10] It said:

> There has to be selection, because we are beginning to create aspirations which society cannot match ... If we have a highly educated and highly idle population we may possibly anticipate more serious social conflict. People must be educated once more to know their place.

In the light of that statement, it is for pragmatic as well as politically sound reasons that the organised working class would do well to acknowledge the leadership and extensive experience at the grass-roots of the black community in the field of educational reform, from which other sections of the working class have been notably absent since the advent of the 1944 Education Act.

Reformed formal structures, however, as the black

community well knows, are no substitute for grass-roots activity, particularly within the framework of a large, unwieldy institution like an education authority which has limited powers to enforce change. That power lies effectively with headteachers and school governors, both of which groups are dismally lacking in black representation. Campaigning work to encourage more black people, especially parents, to become governors is now an important community priority. A London-wide association for black governors was formed in 1986.

The extent to which the composition of school governing bodies can be changed so that they truly reflect the communities and school populations they serve will be a strong influence on the direction of one of the most controversial educational debates to result from the presence of black people in this country: separate black schools. So bitter and disillusioned have many black parents become with the third-rate deal their children have or are likely to receive in state education that some have turned to the private sector and set up their own schools. Many others wish they had the resources to follow suit. Most of the black schools in existence are of religious foundation, such as the John Loughborough School in Haringey, set up by the Seventh Day Adventists, and the Pentecostal Life Christian School in South London. These are first and foremost religious schools which happen to be predominantly black, although a handful of white pupils also attend. They are run along educationally traditional lines, in the style of an old grammar school, with the emphasis on academic standards and discipline. The children achieve good academic results compared with their peers in state schools. It is extremely difficult to argue against a black parent who opts for such a school, or who calls for specifically black schools to be established, when the alternatives on the whole offer such a hostile environment to black children and even have an educational ethos which conflicts with the wishes of many black parents, whose views on education could be interpreted as retrogressive in terms of opposition to the comprehensive principle. Indeed, many of the values and objectives which black parents seek for their children in schools correspond more closely with those associated with the white middle classes, not the working class at all.

There is an important distinction to be made between black schools and religious schools which happen to be black. The level of demand for black schools is isolated and unrepresentative of the community as a whole.

> The demand for black schools has not really been sustained. In the sixties and seventies, we were aping the US experience and thought black schools and black studies were the answer. I wouldn't support that any more. Separatism is backward and unrealistic. We certainly wouldn't win the support from progressive white people for that position. Religious schools are a different question. Blackness is not a religion.

The Swann report came out against black schools, religious or otherwise. The four West Indians on the committee and others dissented from that conclusion, not out of any allegiance (on my part anyway) to denominational schools but on the principle of equality of treatment under the present law. As long as the law allows religious groups to run their own schools – and a substantial number of Catholics, Anglicans and Jewish people, for example, take advantage of this-freedom – there is no case for making exceptions of religions where they happen to be practised by black communities, be they Seventh Day Adventists, Rastafarians or Moslems. Preferable in practice, however, would be state schools in which children from any religious background could feel they belonged, as they would if there were genuine and vigorous implementation of all the other recommendations of Swann.

The pressure for separate schools also needs to be assessed in the context of demographic changes in many inner-city areas. There are schools which are effectively becoming black schools through natural development. In Hackney in London, for example, black children formed over 60 per cent of the borough's school age population by 1985. If black people were to have their fair share of control and influence, as members of the community through the governing body *and* as members of staff, those 'black' schools would not become the ghetto schools so feared by the education 'experts' in Haringey in 1969, but would become the model of accountability and educational standards desired by all.

Racism and the Labour Movement

Whilst the unity of interest arising out of race and class in the area of education is clear although relatively unexploited, the black struggle against institutional racism in the trade union and labour movement has faced an historical confrontation between race and class. In earlier chapters, the experiences of the fifties immigrants illustrated the impenetrability of trade union colleagues on the questions of race. The class barrier, we were told, needed to be broken down first. The same view was held by both the Labour Party and the Communist Party. In a critique of the traditional Marxist definition of racism, Chris Mullard challenged the class-before-race position succinctly:

> ... race cannot be readily subsumed under class without distorting at least four centuries of British history in order to liken slave labour with wage labour.[11]

Mullard's analysis is echoed in the words of a trade union leader who came to Britain in 1952 from Jamaica and spent many years as a shop steward in the building industry:

> My impression was always that the left was genuinely concerned to mobilise the black community, but into *their* political battles. They never had time to look at *our* immediate problems, so it became futile to refer to them. So blacks ended up in total isolation within the broad left because of the left's basic dishonesty. They still believe they know more. It's an inbuilt prejudice of people born in the country which was our colonial master.

A survey conducted as recently as 1984, commissioned by West Midlands Regional Council of the TUC, revealed a consensus amongst white union officials that black trade unionists lacked either interest in or understanding of trade unionism.[12] Black members complained of the hostility or indifference they experienced in their unions, which they perceived as white organisations completely unprepared to represent their interests or grievances. Black members ended up with 'feelings of isolation, exclusion and helplessness as a minority in a democratic organisation dominated by majority interests'.

Shattering though it may be for white trade unionists, perhaps with many years of experience in the one organisation in their lives where they genuinely feel they share in democratic practice, the fact is that where black people are in a minority that very democracy is oppressive. Democracy cannot be a monolithic structure. Where rules and practices were adopted without black people in mind because they literally were not there, their fairness of operation ceases to exist when black people become part of the structure. But in the face of 'democratic' resistance, black people have had to find their own ways to participate in organisations to whose principles they subscribe and whose objectives they support.

Caucusing has developed as the main way in which black people have asserted their presence in trade unions. This practice has now, by and large, acquired legitimacy and even encouragement within several unions, but not before black members had had to insist that it was their right. An initial response was the equation of caucusing with separatism. But by definition, caucusing assumes a corporate membership of the wider body as a whole. A black caucus simply aims to ensure that that wider body is more fully informed by and answerable to its whole membership. What black trade unionists need to beware of is the tokenistic co-option of a 'black caucus' within the upper echelons of the power hierarchy, cut off from genuine channels of communication with the grass-roots black membership. This would be to subvert the democratising influence of the practice of caucusing. A similar mistake was made by a group of leading black trade unionists themselves when they set up the Black Trade Unionists Solidarity Movement. One who opposed the move says:

Caucusing within trade unions has succeeded in getting black issues on the agenda. It has highlighted both individual and institutional racism. And it has given black trade unionists a sense of purpose. But the Black Trade Unionists Solidarity Movement was misconceived. You can't set up a caucus by an institution. It has to come from the ground. People joined BTUSM like a society, started to jostle for positions. It wasn't long before internal arguments and frustration set in.

It is the activities of trade unionists at their workplace and within their union which will determine the extent to which documents of good intention will ever achieve more than lip-service at national union level. Despite the existence of the TUC's Black Workers Charter (1981) or the model equal opportunities clause, or the CRE's Code of Practice which came into force in April 1984, the GLC's Anti-Racist Trade Union Working Group found in November 1984 that:

> ... blacks, particularly the young, are still cynical and suspicious of the trade union movement, because they believe that the unions have no firm intention of realising those policies where it matters most and that is by fighting racism at the workplace.

Unless trade unions re-assess their priorities, it is alarmingly clear that those young black people who are in work will not necessarily follow their parents' generation loyally into the trade union movement. There will be no obvious reason for them to join. They may be part of the working class but their primary experience is of being black. The trade union movement has to offer them something *as black people* if they are also to identify with what the union has to offer them in terms of their class.

If it is assumed, by an organisation or institution, that no specific initiatives need to be taken on account of racism or black people, on the grounds that the interests of black people are no different from the interests of the working class as a whole, it follows that any organisational initiative by black members is automatically seen as divisive. This has been the experience of the black Labour Party members campaigning for black sections within the party as well as of various groups of black trade unionists. What this reflects on the part of the white people in control is a denial of their own historical legacy and cultural heritage of struggle as members of the trade union and labour movement. No advance towards democracy or socialism was ever handed to the working class on a plate; it had to be won in struggle. This is not to say that struggle has disappeared from the life of the labour movement. On the contrary, under the Thatcher government there have been struggles on such a scale and of so fundamental a nature that we may have cause to hope that they will assist in developing a closer understanding of both the scale and specific qualities of the black struggle. There were certainly signs of this during the miners' strike in 1984-85 when the miners' experience of police harassment awakened a level of solidarity with the black community's daily experience which had, up to then, been an unthinkable experience for the miners.

This identification of experience and interests, however, is relatively uncommon across the labour movement as a whole. What those opposed to black sections are saying is, they are unnecessary, we're already fighting racism, we stand for everyone, black or white. In other words, we are here comfortably in control, don't rock the boat. It must genuinely be painful for the leadership of the labour movement to be subjected to such a public challenge to their authority to speak for black people, to whom they genuinely believe they are committed. But no struggle is free of contradictions and this is one of them. Their pain and discomfort pales beside the experience which black people carry inside us of slavery, followed by colonialism, followed by racist exclusion from participation in a democratic society. That is the brutal comparison which has to be acknowledged. The conflict between the campaign for black sections in the Labour Party and the party's leadership has to be interpreted historically as a conflict which can lead to a better outcome for both black and white people.

There is not unanimity amongst black people over the need for black sections and the white leadership has been able to draw on the differences which naturally arise within the black perspective to fuel its own unprincipled opposition. The leadership unfortunately has one star witness to call on in Bill Morris, Deputy General Secretary of the Transport and General Workers' Union, the only black trade unionist in such a senior position. In an article in the *Morning Star* he reiterated the view that black sections are both 'sectarian' and 'divisive'.[13] Other black activists of long standing within the labour movement express more thoughtful reservation:

In an ideal world, black sections wouldn't be necessary. But the need has arisen through lack of opportunity. In reality, black people have always had to organise within the white mainstream. They need to now, within the Labour Party. And if they joined the Communist Party, they'd have to do the same there. The danger is that black sections could turn into a political ghetto for black people. A lot will depend on their leadership.

Black sections run the risk of marginalising the struggle for race equality, which is not just about black people needing a route into certain positions. I need convincing that black sections in the Labour Party will raise issues, not just personalities. We shouldn't need black sections to say that aspiring black politicians need safe seats. The racism within the Labour Party has created black sections, but I worry about them taking away the edge to the struggle by concentrating on the issue of representation.

We need black MPs, but not if they're going to turn into bulwarks of the black middle class.

These statements pose some important questions for the black sections campaigners to address, as indeed they have begun to through their actions. Their campaign slogan, 'Registration, Recruitment and Representation', illustrated that their work is not purely in their own interests as potential MPs, but also for the benefit of their party (recruitment) and in order to increase the chance of a Labour victory at the next General Election (registration). A campaign launched at the end of 1983 in Hackney, for example, aimed to increase the registration of black people eligible to vote. 30 per cent of the borough's eligible black population of about 30,000 were not on the electoral roll.

As for racism inside the Labour Party as an organisation and in terms of its policies, black sections are not all that is needed. The Labour Party cannot exempt itself from the process of dismantling institutional racism. It purports to be a party which expresses change, so it cannot place itself outside that change. It would be all too easy for black sections to be seen as the place where issues of race are dealt with, without allowing that black perspective to influence the wider party. This marginalisation has been precisely what the women's sections have had to strive to overcome. A black perspective is needed not only on policies concerning racism and black people, but on all issues. Anti-racist committees or advisories, consisting of both black and white party members should complement but not undermine or overshadow black sections.

By the same token, black members who opt to be active in black sections must be seen to be making the political links between racism and other key policy areas which should form the bedrock of what the Labour Party stands for: an alternative social and economic strategy, peace and disarmament, international solidarity. A minority exercising its equal right to participate would be injecting into the Labour Party new ideas and new forms of organisation which could enhance its appeal. At present, black people are not part of the machinery, or any machinery in society. We are therefore not conservative in the sense that most white British people are, for we cannot take any institution for granted.

Yet herein lies another link between the long experience of the black community and the experience which has more recently and suddenly hit the mass of British people under Thatcherism: institutions which have been taken for granted are being attacked or dismantled under our noses. The health service, the social security system, the trade union movement, public services such as gas and water, all have been subject to attack by legislative restrictions or privatisation, to an extent that individuals' ability to participate in society and control their own lives and standard of living has been reduced, not extended as Mrs Thatcher would have us believe.

If the white working class can understand that the degree of alienation from the structures of society which it is now experiencing has always been the experience of the black community, then it may be more willing to be informed by the black community and look to it for leadership rather than for the nearest scapegoat. For the Labour Party not to throw away this chance provided by Thatcherism to be instrumental in forging a real ideological unity between the black and white communities in Britain, it must accept – and welcome – black sections.

Activists in black sections have been criticised for being out of contact with the black community. The fear that the black Members of Parliament this country will undoubtedly soon have will be no more than black middle-class individuals pursuing a career flows from that criticism. The onus of preventing this falls equally on their shoulders and the community as a whole. A broad-based national black organisation, which could possibly be developed out of the existing structure of the West Indian Standing Conference and similar bodies within the Asian community, is now a more urgent requirement than ever before. Many previous attempts to set up such a national forum have failed. But the present political scenario demands an organised national expression of the black community, not only for the benefit of white policy-makers, but as a structure for the accountability of black leaders to their own community. This goes for the black individuals who are going to become leaders in the business world just as much as the political world. West Indians *are* joining the Tory Party too. And the Tory Cabinet has made it clear in the wake of the 1985 uprisings in Brixton, Handsworth and Tottenham, that part of its strategy to contain black politics is to play midwife to an Afro-Caribbean middle class. We have to ensure that successful black business-people set the pace in community accountability just as we have in the field of the education service, and do not get hijacked by 'popular capitalism'. The allure of the success of black capitalism in the United States is attractive, but the lessons are already there to be learned.

The American Experience

The American black rights movement has not yet succeeded in shifting material wealth to the vast majority of the black population, because of the success of the establishment in buying off their black brokers, who have become, in the words of black Communist Harry Heywood in his autobiography *Black Bolshevik*, a 'black internal colony, still owned and controlled by white monopoly capitalism'.[14]

I had a personal insight into this phenomenon in 1980 when I went as an observer from the Caribbean Teachers' Association to the Annual Convention of the National Urban League of America. The League is a predominantly black organisation funded mainly by white liberal institutions which carry out race relations work. The convention took place during the last few days of the Presidential election. Thousands of delegates attended from all over the United States. The venue was the Sheraton Hotel on Fifth Avenue in New York. It was such an impressive occasion that all four Presidential candidates found it necessary to attend to deliver keynote speeches. There was very little opposition from the delegates to anything they said. What little murmur of disagreement did surface was quickly and firmly removed from the hall by the security people in abundance.

I had gone to the convention eager with anticipation to hear exciting discussion on the state of black America. The lack of contention astonished me. During the only real discussion that took place, predictably in the bar in the evenings, it dawned on me what had really happened. Most of the delegates sported their identification badges, informing us that they were Presidents or Vice-Presidents of this or that community organisation, or, in many cases, of prestigious business organisations. Many of these organisations were state-funded and these people were clearly not prepared to risk their new-found status and livelihoods. The important thing I discovered was that many of these people had been activists in the heyday of the civil rights movement. They had discarded their ideological conviction along with their former style of dress. No more Afros. WASPish three-piece suits in place of dashikis. And rimless spectacles replaced by the no-bullshit horn-rimmed ones. This was the black middle class created by white America in its own interests.

It seems to me that they need to take a great deal of care not to betray the interests of their less fortunate brothers and sisters whose struggles have opened up the space for a few individuals to occupy positions of apparent authority. It is not in the interests of those who still live in poverty in the blighted inner city to lose their leadership.

This containment of black aspiration to equality left the door open to a ferocious white backlash, the resurgence of fascist groups and the undermining of the artificially created black middle class. This is a lesson to be learned now by our black community in Britain. It does not have to happen. The fate of a struggle for race equality which is not underpinned by – underpinned by, not subordinate to – class politics is as clear for Britain as it has been for the United States. The difference between the 'middle-class' success which it would be churlish not to wish for anyone in the black community, and the middle class which consigns itself to a 'black internal colony' was expressed with acute perception by a young black man interviewed by the *Sunday Times* in 1985 for a colour supplement feature on 'Britain's new middle class'. 'You're looking for the black middle class?' he said, 'Which one do you mean? The middle class in the black community or the black people in the white middle class?'

In *Black Bolshevik*, Harry Heywood said that a new wave of black activists must strive to 'recapture their revolutionary heritage'. The same imperative must apply to the generation of black activists in Britain who are currently engaging in battle on the streets. Revolutionary they are, but only in an immediate and directionless fashion, if the tension and oppression which sparks off the flashpoints of confrontation is not allied either to an understanding of their heritage as activists or to a vision of the kind of society they could help to achieve. Their predecessors in struggle amongst the generation of fifties immigrants became disillusioned with the organised left, but they did not lose their conviction for a socialist future. Black capitalism cannot offer a solution to the unemployment, poverty and marginalisation of the vast majority of black people in society. As in the United States, black capitalism here can empower individuals, but not the communities they come from. In Britain, it is only within the socialist tradition that the commitment to popular power, equality of opportunity and the systematic redistribution of material wealth is found. All these objectives coincide with the demands and objective interests of the black community. So, although racism pre-dates capitalism and post-dates socialism at its current stages of development around the world, the objectives of socialism (not just in political and economic terms, but in the way human beings relate to one another) reflect the aspirations of both the working class movement and the black movement in Britain.

A Dream Intact

This chapter has pointed to some of the concrete bases for a working alliance between the black community and the left and labour movement. Socialism as our goal must underwrite that alliance. In the context of contemporary British politics, the immediate goals concern the extension of democracy and the fight against inequalities which lie at the heart of the battle against racism. In other words, no socialist movement can call itself such unless it includes black people as equal partners. And no socialist movement can afford to do without the black community amongst its forces of leadership.

Part of the socialist and anti-racist consciousness of the white left must be to accept the suspicion and bitterness of the black community towards it, which springs from the left's traditional tendency to colonise black support for political priorities it has not been allowed to help determine. Most black people believe in making alliances. The difficulty is in being equal within those alliances. At the moment, there is a black agenda and a white agenda. Two black Communist Party activists of long standing see ways of bringing the agendas closer together:

> I can't see race in pure class terms. If you interpret the broad democratic alliance correctly, then alliance with black groups have to be with them *as black*. But the party is dragging its feet on this. Some of our black comrades left the party because they felt it wasn't reaching *out* to the black community, even though its politics were right.

> The idea of the broad democratic alliance is a difficult one to sell to the black community. Talk about unity is often seen as an excuse to avoid the immediate, specific issues which black people want sorting out. Black people want to involve the whole community, but get frustrated when the left comes in, because they see the impact of the left in terms of suppressing, not activating, the community. The only way to get it across is to be stronger about saying that socialism is the goal of the broad democratic alliance. We have to convince the black community that we are after a changed system.

The current version of the Communist Party's programme, *The British Road to Socialism*, has moved a long way from the head-in-the-sand politics of the early fifties, still clouded by colonialism. But it is frustrating and sad that the only political party which now seems to understand in theory the links between anti-racism and democracy, and between socialism and black liberation, should be the very party which lost the allegiance of so many committed black socialists by not listening to them when it had the chance.

The words quoted above are by people who may have had some illusions about life in Britain shattered, but who continue, through their political and ideological commitment, to have a dream intact. The struggle ahead is about recreating and passing on that dream, about an equal and rewarding life for all. The door to the road to socialism is still open for anyone prepared to go through it and embark – or re-embark – on that journey. It is only by being brave enough to swim against the stream that we can turn attitudes around. When my generation came to Britain, we were hated for being black and resented for being British. When our children and grandchildren can feel proud of being both and accepted for being both, the illusion of my generation will have become a reality.

Notes

1. C. Gutzmore, 'The Notting Hill Carnival', *Marxism Today*, August 1982.
2. Quoted in Roisin Boyd, 'Black Women under white-law', *Spare Rib*, July 1982.
3. West Indian Standing Conference, Minutes of Consultation on Urban Disturbances, Handsworth, 19 October 1985.
4. See for example, *Immigrant Housing*, GLC Research Library, 1976; *Colour and the allocation of GLC housing*, GLC Research Report 21, 1976; T. Taper, 'The allocation of Islington housing to ethnic minorities', *New Community*, Vol. 6, No. 1/2 (Winter 1977/8); *Race and Council Housing in Hackney*, Commission for Racial Equality, 1984.
5. J. Rex and S. Tomlinson, *Colonial Immigrants in a British City – A Class Analysis*, Routledge, 1979.
6. *Birmingham Local Education Authority and Schools – referral and suspension of pupils*, CRE, April 1985.
7. C. Mullard, *Racism in Society and Schools: History, Policy and Practice*, Centre for MultiCultural Education, University of London Institute of Education, 1980.
8. *West Indian Children in our Schools*, Cmnd 8273, HMSO, 1981.
9. *Education for All*, the report of the Committee for Enquiry into the Education of Children from Ethnic Minority Groups, Cmnd 9453, HMSO, 1985.
10. S. Ranson, 'Towards a Tertiary Tripartism: New Codes of Social Control and the 17+' in Patricia Broadfoot (ed.), *Selection, Certification and Control*, London, 1984.
11. Mullard, op.cit.
12. Dr. G. Lee, *Trade Unionism and Race*, reported in *Employment Report*, CRE, January 1985.
13. *Morning Star*, 26 November 1985.
14. H. Heywood, *Black Bolshevik, Autobiography of an Afro-American Communist*, Liberator Press, Chicago, Illinois, 1978.

Index